DOOLITTLE

SERIES EDITOR
Dennis E. Showalter, Ph.D.
Colorado College

Instructive summaries for general and expert readers alike, volumes in the Military Profiles series are essential treatments of significant and popular military figures drawn from world history, ancient times through the present.

DOOLITTLE

Aerospace Visionary

Dik Alan Daso

BRASSEY'S, INC.
Washington, D.C.

Library of Congress Cataloging-in-Publication Data
Daso, Dik A., 1959–
    Doolittle, aerospace visionary / Dik Alan Daso.
        p. cm.— (Military profiles)
Includes bibliographical references and index.
    ISBN 1-57488-420-4 (hardcover : alk. paper)
1. Doolittle, James Harold, 1896–1993 2. Air pilots—United States—Biography. 3. Generals—United States—Biography. 4. United States. Army Air Forces—Biography. 5. Aeronautics—United States—History. I. Title. II. Series.
    TL540.D62D37 2003
    629.13'092—dc21

                                                            2003007787

Hardcover ISBN 1-57488-420-4
(alk. paper)

Printed in the United States of America on acid-free paper that meets the American National Standards Institute z39-48 Standard.

Brassey's, Inc.
22841 Quicksilver Drive
Dulles, Virginia 20166

FIRST EDITION

10 9 8 7 6 5 4 3 2 1

Contents

Maps

Preface

One hundred years ago, man flew for the first time in a powered, winged contraption. Since Orville and then Wilbur left the sands of Kitty Hawk on 17 December 1903, the evolution of aviation and the technology associated with flying have taken mankind from the windswept beaches of North Carolina to the dusty desolation of the moon. From bailing wire and fabric to solid magnesium and ultrastrong composites, air- and spacecraft have been part of what most agree is a revolution in how we live our daily lives. Travel across vast reaches of territory that once took months on foot and horseback now takes hours in commercial airliners. Regions not routinely visited at the turn of the twentieth century, like Alaska, are now as accessible as any major city. Families, once geographically collocated, are today linked not by distance but by time. Overnight and electronic mail facilitate commerce around the world. Our earth is not as vast as it once was.

Military battles once fought in close quarters are now often fought half a world away from adversaries; weapons are launched from afar with increasingly deadly, if yet not perfect, precision. Those who wish only to do harm have blurred the lines between military and civil aviation. The development of the science and technology related to aeronautics and space sciences has accelerated with the advent of incredibly powerful computational capability. On a list of great names in American aviation history, there are none whose lives entwine with the aerospace-science and aviation-technology revolution more completely, and on such a broad scale, than James Harold Doolittle (1896–1993).

I have long thought that a new, critical examination of James H. "Jimmy" Doolittle's career and lifelong influence upon both military and civil aeronautical science and technology was needed. Unfortunately, this is not that book. Why? Simple. Thirty-five thousand words are not enough to critically detail this near-centurion aviator's life. But it is a first step—an introduction—to the wide range of Doolittle's contributions and how his many remarkable achievements have influenced the development of American airpower. At Brassey's request, this biography covers the "essentials," of a remarkable career in academe, industry, and military service. That said, I believe the reader will profit from fresh interpretation of Doolittle's early flying career, a revised examination of the Tokyo Raid, and the addition of a few new sources and photographs that are published in this work for the first time.

Doolittle is a fertile project. Although his primary biographer, Carroll V. Glines, has addressed much of his life's activity, and done so admirably, critical evaluation of Doolittle's relationship to the evolution of American airpower has been clouded by admiration and myth. The linkage between a human being and the development of a technological system that has evolved into a metasystem over the past century is not only intriguing but also trendy as far as historical scholarship goes.

Doolittle's participation in that evolutionary process—one of system building—exists on many levels. He was a pioneer aviator, flying airplanes before many Americans had even seen one. He participated in the development of military aviation, both doctrinally and technically. He "pushed the edge of the envelope" as a test pilot, taming racing aircraft that kept even his most skilled contemporaries hugging the ground. He spent many years in civil aviation as a salesman and test pilot.

In addition to actual piloting, he was an air-combat leader. He developed a knack for recognizing how to accomplish tasks and then carefully executing plans—from the famous raid on Tokyo to massive B-17 attacks on Germany during the Second World War. He grew from a combat pilot into a skilled, creative air-combat commander.

After the war, he put the totality of his experiences to good use while serving on any number of science panels, technology boards, and advocacy groups. He spent the second half of his ninety-six years doling out the experience he had gained during the first half of his life. He held positions of great influence in the scientific and technical communities, and it is here that his story remains underdeveloped. I cannot fully rectify that shortcoming in these pages, but someday I will.

Although a full-length critical biography is a few years away, it seemed appropriate, a decade after Doolittle's death, to offer this concise overview as part of the centennial of the Wright brothers' first manned flight at Kitty Hawk.

I would like to thank Carlo D'Este for examining the manuscript. As a fellow biographer, he offered a critical perspective of and gifted insight into Doolittle's relationship with George Patton, the subject of much of his work. Also, to my friend and colleague Phil Meilinger, who meticulously read and provided analytical comments on the completed manuscript, I owe much. His eye for detail saved me from otherwise unrecognized errors in style and substance. Additionally, I owe a significant debt of gratitude to Carroll V. "CV" Glines, who graciously evaluated the manuscript and provided insight that only his long-term association with Doolittle and the Raiders could. All errors in this volume are my own.

Chronology

1896	Born, Alameda, California, December 14. Parents Rosa and Frank Doolittle.
1900	Family moves to Nome, Alaska.
1908	Rosa and Jimmy return to Southern California.
1917	Enlists in Army Signal Corps (Air Service), October. Marries Josephine E. "Joe" Daniels in Los Angeles, Christmas Eve.
1918	Completes flight training, commissioned 2d Lieutenant in the Signal Reserve, Aviation Section.
1921	Participates in Billy Mitchell's bombardment tests off the Virginia coast.
1922	First transcontinental flight (Florida to California) in less than twenty-four hours flying a modified DH-4B.
1923	Enters Massachusetts Institute of Technology, earns master's and doctorate by June 1925.
1925	Wins Schneider Marine Cup Race for floatplanes only. Awarded Mackay Trophy along with Cy Bettis, winner of the Pulitzer Race, for most outstanding military flight of the year.
1927	First pilot to execute an outside loop.
1929	First blind landing accomplished at Mitchel Field, New York. Funded by the Guggenheims. Belated award of the Distinguished Flying Cross for 1922 transcontinental flight and aeronautical studies while at MIT.

1930   Leaves Army and begins working for Shell
          Petroleum as an aviation product representative.

1931   Wins Bendix Trophy flying a Laird Super Solution
          from California to Cleveland, continued to New
          York, setting a west-to-east transcontinental record:
          first to cross in less than twelve hours.

1932   Wins Thompson Race flying the dangerous
          Granville GeeBee, R-1.

1934   Shell, at Doolittle's insistence, produces first batch of
          hundred-octane aviation fuel. Doolittle serves on the
          Baker Board, offering the only dissenting opinion.

1940   Hap Arnold calls Doolittle back into Army Air
          Corps as a member of his staff.

1942   Leads sixteen North American B-25B "Mitchell"
          bombers in a daring carrier-launched raid against
          Tokyo, April 18. Promoted to brigadier general,
          skipping over colonel. Awarded the Medal of
          Honor for heroism in leading the mission.
          Assigned as commander of Twelfth Air Force,
          North Africa. Promoted to major general.

1943   Casablanca Conference establishes the Combined
          Bomber Offensive (CBO) as the method for air at-
          tacks against Germany. Doolittle assigned as com-
          manding general of Fifteenth Air Force, Italy.

1944   Promoted to lieutenant general and made
          commanding general of Eighth Air Force, England.
          Turns fighters loose on the Luftwaffe and
          spearheads "Big Week," the air battle that turned
          the tide of the air war.

1945   Commanding general, Eighth Air Force, Okinawa.
          Present on the deck of the *Missouri* during the un-
          conditional surrender of the Japanese.

1946   Leaves military service, becomes the first president
          of the Air Force Association. Returns to Shell
          Union Oil as vice president (1946–47) and director
          (1946–67).

1947	The Air Force becomes a separate service.
1953	Chairman, 50th Anniversary of Powered Flight.
1955	Chairman, USAF Scientific Advisory Board (1955–58). Member, President's Foreign Intelligence Advisory Board (1955–65).
1956	Chairman, National Advisory Committee for Aeronautics (NACA, 1956–58)
1958	Son, James Jr., commits suicide, April.
1959	Director, Space Technologies Laboratories (1959–63).
1961	Director, Mutual of Omaha Insurance Company (1961–86).
1966	Inducted into the International Space Hall of Fame, San Diego, California.
1967	Thomas D. White National Defense Award. Inducted into the Aviation Hall of Fame, Dayton, Ohio.
1988	Joe Doolittle dies of complications from a stroke, Christmas Eve.
1989	George H. W. Bush awards Doolittle the Presidential Medal of Freedom.
1991	Publishes autobiography, *I Could Never Be So Lucky Again.*
1993	Dies on September 27 in son John's Pebble Beach, California, home at the age of ninety-six.

DOOLITTLE

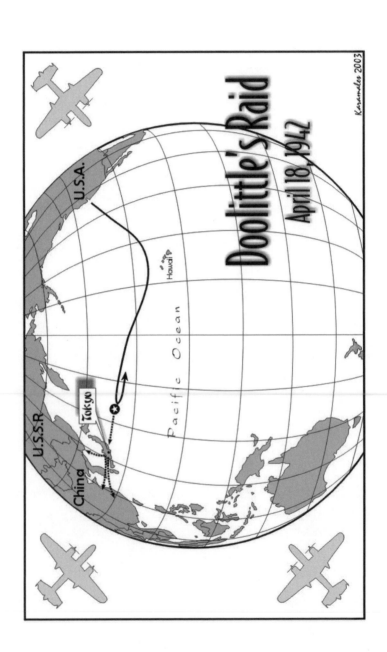

Doolittle's Raid
April 18, 1942

U.S.A.

U.S.S.R.

China

Tokyo

Hawaii

Pacific Ocean

Kesander 2003

Chapter 1

Tough Upbringing

Doolittle was born on 14 December 1896 in Alameda, California, just across the bay from San Francisco. His first and middle names were decided upon some days after his birth. James Harold Doolittle was the only child of Frank Henry Doolittle, a skilled carpenter, and Rosa Ceremah Shephard, an outdoors type and disciplinarian. Soon after James's birth, Frank took his tools and went north, following the promise of easy money in Alaska. Not yet four years old, young James, his mother, and her sister Sarah joined Frank in Nome, Alaska, in the summer of 1900. The smallest boy in the new Nome grammar school, Doolittle was a constant target for bullies. "I had to fight all the time," he remembered.[1]

Doolittle's family photo album tells a graphic story of his early life. The schoolhouse was a medium-size room with a pot-bellied stove in the middle for warmth. In photos, the children were stoic—not so much as a smirk emanating from their stone-cold faces.[2] Perhaps it was the continual fist fighting between young men, such as Doolittle and his adversaries, that forced the strict environment.

Outside of school, Doolittle enjoyed "manly" pursuits. Encouraged by his father, he took an interest in carpentry. He participated in one of the few sports available in the town—marathon running. Additionally, he took up tumbling and acrobatics, skills he carried with him through college. Rosa Doolittle filled the family album with pictures of long-distance races through the streets of Nome and of her only son striking acrobatic poses alone and in uniformed groups of three. Handstands and formations demonstrating extreme strength filled the album.[3]

Although small and wiry in build, Doolittle was pure muscle. He was in trouble often enough as a youngster that when he was wrongly accused of damaging a neighbor's property, his father punished him and accused him of lying after he denied any involvement in the affair. The incident added pressure to their already tenuous father-son relationship. Doolittle recalled, "I didn't lie then and I don't lie now."[4] This childhood honesty translated into adult integrity, one of Doolittle's most powerful character traits.

In the summer of 1908, Rosa and James left Nome for Southern California. Why James's father remained up north was never clear, but Frank continued to practice his trade. It was two years later, in the clear skies at Dominguez Field, near Los Angeles, that thirteen-year-old Jimmy Doolittle was introduced to the infant science of aviation and aircraft technology. Famous airmen had traveled across the country in an attempt to win a $20,000 prize for setting new aviation records. Attending this first air meet west of the mighty Mississippi River were Glenn H. Curtiss, a no-nonsense motorcycle builder turned airplane engine manufacturer; Roy A. Knabenshue, an early aerial showman; and a representative from the Wright Aircraft Company, Arch Hoxsey, who flew the Wright B Flyer during the meet.[5]

This was the first life-altering event in Doolittle's young life. He had found his calling, although it would be eight more years before he realized his dream of flying like those he saw soaring above the California crowds.

Meanwhile, using his carpentry skills, Doolittle built his own unsuccessful man-size glider from plans printed in *Popular Mechanics*. He took a beating during his attempts to launch the craft—physically and in the area of pride. After his glider became damaged beyond repair, he decided to take up a more traditional form of physical punishment—boxing.

Doolittle's high school English teacher, Forest Bailey, taught him both the physical and the mental art of boxing. Doolittle was strong but angry and fought with rage rather than restraint. Bailey turned the five-foot-four-inch, 105-pound Doolittle, who frequently fought professionally under the name Jimmy Pierce, into an amateur champ. He used his skills to earn money, but every so often he regressed to street brawls. At least once, fighting outside the ring landed Jimmy in the local pokey. His mother once left him there for an entire weekend in an attempt to teach him the value and importance of self-restraint.

It was not until he won the affections of Josephine E. Daniels, a cultured southern belle from Louisiana, that he actually began applying the lessons his mother had been teaching him all along. "There is no doubt that Joe changed my life," Doolittle recalled. "I began to comb my hair, wear a tie, look after my clothes, and watch my language around her." Having Joe by his side became the second life-altering event in Doolittle's youth. Jimmy called it "being domesticated."[6]

Jimmy continued boxing for money. There was no other way for him to earn the cash he needed to take Joe out on dates from time to time. When she rebuked him during his senior year of high school and refused to talk to him because of his propensity to pummel others, he gave in and quit the sport—for the money, anyway. Jimmy promised Joe that he would go to Alaska and land a job after he graduated from Los Angeles Manual Arts High School in 1914.

After an unrewarding year living and working with his father, now in Seward, Alaska, Jimmy returned penniless to Los Angeles as a stowaway on a transport ship. He immediately enrolled at Los Angeles Junior College, where he studied the basic sciences before enrolling at California's School of Mines at Berkeley. While there, Doolittle joined the collegiate boxing team and practiced gymnastics. He had bulked up to a full 130 pounds. Between semesters and during the summer months each of his three years at the School of Mines, he worked at regional mines, like the Comstock Lode, performing the backbreaking labor associated with mining in those days.

Doolittle never lost a boxing match—that is, until May 1917. A more experienced boxer outclassed Jimmy. After this defeat, Doolittle recognized that schooling was a bit more important than boxing. He committed himself to completing his work at the School of Mines. He did not consider the possibility of America's direct involvement in and above the trenches that had scarred Europe since 1914.

Just before his senior year, he volunteered for duty in the Army's Signal Corps. Doolittle and thousands of other young men were informed that after a short delay, they would be sent for pilot training. He was formally enlisted on 6 October 1917 and immediately began ground school at the University of California, Berkeley, flight school. Jimmy never returned to finish his undergraduate engineering degree. His life soared along a different path, an aviation path, from that day forward.

It was during these months of ground school that the rough-and-tumble Jimmy convinced the prim-and-proper Joe to join him in marriage. On Christmas Eve 1917, the couple met at city hall in Los Angeles and were married under civil law by the clerk of the court. Joe paid the fee. So began a seventy-year love affair. Joe stayed in Los Angeles while Jimmy moved to Rockwell Field on North Island, San Diego, for basic flight training.

*   *   *   *

Doolittle's first flight introduced him to the tremendous hazards of early flying. Two "Jennies" collided over the airfield just as Charles Todd, Jimmy's instructor pilot (IP), taxied their JN-4 to the takeoff zone. Todd shut down the engine, and even before Jimmy had flown his first military flight, he and Todd were pulling dead and injured airmen from a burning heap. As was common practice in those dangerous days, Doolittle and his IP climbed back into their Jenny and completed the mission. Doolittle wrote about that first flight, saying, "My love of flying began on that day during that hour."[7] Building a mechanism for dealing with the sudden death associated with flying airplanes also began that same day.

After seven hours and four minutes of flight instruction, Doolittle soloed for the first time. Flight instruction, however, did not end until each student mastered many additional skills. Lessons in acrobatics; loops, rolls, spins, and recoveries; close-formation flying; and navigation and cross-country missions were practiced and mastered. In essence, these are the same skills perfected by those trained in American military flight schools to-day. Only the planes are different. More than half of those who began training in ground school did not earn their wings. In March 1918, Doolittle completed his flight training and was commissioned as a second lieutenant in the Signal Reserve, Aviation Section.

His first flying assignment took him to Lake Charles, Louisiana, where he taught other young pilots how to fly the Thomas-Morse S-4C Scout. A powerful Gulf Coast hurricane arrived unannounced early that fall and decimated the force of three hundred training aircraft. Doolittle was reassigned to Rockwell Field, relieved to be returning to Southern California. Joe was still in Los Angeles.

It was during that tour of duty that Doolittle blossomed as a pilot. He mastered the skills needed by every flight instructor: perfect acrobatics, accurate navigation, and precise formation flying. He recognized the seriousness of instructor duty. He later recalled, "I stuck to the curriculum and didn't take kindly to any student trying to show off or get smart. I wanted them to emulate my seriousness about flying. . . . I wanted to impress on them that flying is serious business and is unforgiving of carelessness, incapacity, or neglect."[8]

Doolittle's litany, likely delivered many times to his students, was a necessary part of their training. After a solo student flying a Thomas-Morse Scout nearly knocked Jimmy and one of his students out of the sky in a midair collision during a landing approach, the realities of early flying and the nature of death in the air became much more personal. In that incident, the propeller on Doolittle's Jenny had cleanly severed the head of the solo student. Jimmy belly-landed the Jenny (the undercarriage had ripped from the craft during the collision), grabbed his student, loaded him into another Jenny, and flew another training mission. On a different day, having just taken off and still low to the ground, Jimmy's propeller sliced the tail off another solo student's aircraft, sending him crashing to his death near the edge of the airfield.[9]

During these years, although he understood the serious consequences of flight training, Jimmy often violated the very principles he taught his students. Doolittle was a natural flyer: gifted in an aircraft. But in his early years in the cockpit, he was sometimes impulsive in the air and made mistakes in aerial judgment that endangered lives and destroyed thousands of dollars worth of government and private property. It was, in fact, only his innate ability that kept him alive until he outgrew his penchant for youthful recklessness.

Not until some years later would he mature enough to recognize the crucial nature of preflight planning and calculation. Doolittle, later in life, recalled his lack of flight discipline with nonchalance: "I admit to being a bit of a mischief maker and am guilty of having a little fun in an airplane. One incident during this period reminds me of my stupidity."[10] On that occasion, Jimmy buzzed two soldiers walking down a road. He flew over them so low that his aircraft struck one on the head, knocking him to the ground. Miraculously, the soldier was not killed. Doolittle, now witness to the flattened man, tried to land his plane nearby. Distracted by the thought that he might have just killed a young man during a practical joke, he flew too close to a fence during his landing, caught a wheel in the wires, and crashed his plane as well. Although crashes were more frequent during these pioneering days, accidents that resulted from "stunting" infuriated commanding officers. Doolittle was grounded for one month and restricted to the post—a mere slap on the wrist by today's disciplinary standards—for lapses in air judgment.

For Jimmy, there were other such lapses. Shortly following the "soldier strike," Doolittle was filmed riding on the landing-gear strut while the pilot accomplished a safe landing. His commander, Colonel Burwell, knew it was Doolittle by reputation alone. Jimmy was an aerial loose cannon during these years. Even on the ground, Jimmy staged stunts that, to most pilots, were dangerous and demonstrated less-than-perfect judgment. He once flew an aircraft through the open doors of an aircraft hangar just to help the mechanics sweep the place out. One day, while grounded for that infraction, he drove his motorcycle into the path of a landing Scout aircraft. The angry pilot tried to land again, and Doolittle thwarted that attempt as well. In disgust, the pilot flew to the other end of the airfield and landed. Colonel Burwell was that pilot, and Doolittle remained confined for an additional month.[11]

In another incident, Doolittle and a friend were chasing a flock of migrating waterfowl through a mountain pass. While concentrating on the birds, he flew into a valley too steep for the underpowered Jenny to handle. He crashed the plane on the top of a ridge, narrowly escaping serious injury—another wreck caused by inattention, carelessness, and an incomplete understanding of his aircraft's technical capabilities. Doolittle was correct, though: Mistakes in the air often resulted in unforgiving consequences. He was fortunate to have suffered only a few facial scars as a result of his escapades.[12]

When the war ended at 11 A.M. on 11 November 1918, Doolittle was forced to decide whether or not to remain in the Army. He was influenced during an air meet, much like the first one that introduced Jimmy to airplanes in 1910. This time, however, Lieutenant Doolittle was a flying participant, not a spectator. A member of the Rockwell low-flying team (the equivalent of the USAF Thunderbirds or the Navy's Blue Angels), he was among the hundreds of planes soaring over a field in celebration of victory in the First World War. The *Los Angeles Times* reported, "So close to one and other [*sic*] that they seemed almost to touch, they formed a ceiling over the sky that almost blotted out the struggling rays of the sun . . . the five acrobats below swooped, dived, looped and spun in perfect unison as though they had been operated by a single hand."[13]

The military paycheck was nice, but he loved flying and the roar of a huge crowd was overwhelming—an ego builder. Doolittle stayed.

Chapter 2

Reputation Building

T HE GREAT WAR over, the American military establishment began to demobilize its forces. Thousands of soldiers and sailors returned to civilian life. Many of those who remained in the service were transferred to new assignments. Doolittle moved to Kelly Field, near San Antonio, Texas, where he was immediately restricted to the post for "stunting" a DH-4 Jenny.

By October 1919, punishments now served, Jimmy was reassigned to the Ninetieth Aero Squadron, located at Eagle Pass, Texas, on the Rio Grande. There he participated in extensive border-patrol activities. The Ninetieth held responsibility for the entire southern border, from Brownsville, at the southern tip of Texas, all the way to San Diego, California. The land was unforgiving, unbearably hot most of the time, and breathtakingly beautiful—at least in west Texas. Although the mission was somewhat broad, the flying offered tremendous opportunity to experiment. Flying under the Pecos River Bridge, one of the highest rail bridges then in existence, was common sport for the pilots.

After a few months of patrolling, the missions became mundane. Jimmy decided to send for Joe, who moved from San

Diego to join him. The boredom and the onset of miserable Texas flying weather in January and February led to idle hands, and children. By the time Jimmy and Joe had been reassigned to Kelly Field in July 1920, she was pregnant, Jimmy was promoted to first lieutenant, and they moved into officer quarters that seemed palatial after the "early Air Service" decor they had left behind on the border. James Jr. was born on 2 October 1920.[1]

While at the mechanics' school, Doolittle was taught by the professionals, no tinkering anymore. He received hands-on experience under the watchful eye of these skilled technicians, training that paid big benefits later in his career. As a pilot, he also had the opportunity to fly captured enemy aircraft. Jimmy was broadening his knowledge of American and foreign technology by learning and doing. "This assignment would prove to be a milestone in my life," he later wrote.[2] As it turned out, this assignment was only the first of many important career milestones.

In May 1921, Doolittle was temporarily assigned to Langley Field, Virginia, where he trained for a significant demonstration of airpower potential. Commanded by the outspoken Gen. William "Billy" Mitchell, Air Service bombers sunk captured German ships to demonstrate the tenuous survivability of battleships. "We flew practice missions in the DH-4s almost daily. . . . I participated in one mission bombing the destroyer and another going after the submarine . . . but I don't recall that we did much damage." Photographic evidence revealed the actual damage during later aerial bombardment tests. Mitchell's point was made on 21 July 1921, when the *Ostfriesland*, considered unsinkable by many in the Navy, went to the bottom. The Air Brigade was disbanded, and Doolittle returned to Kelly Field.[3]

Jimmy returned to another pregnancy. Joe gave birth to their second son, John Prescott, on 29 June 1922. While enjoying his newborn, Jimmy began planning the first of many record-breaking aerial achievements. He requested permission to fly coast to coast in less than twenty-four hours, a feat not yet accomplished. This transcontinental flight proved to be a major turning point for the sometimes impulsive aviator.

Under direct scrutiny of the chief of the Air Service, Maj. Gen. Mason M. Patrick, and recognizing the deleterious public consequences of failure, Doolittle spent weeks planning, test-flying, and modifying his DH-4B to facilitate success. He realized that what he had proposed was not like wing-walking or flying under a bridge. Large numbers of people were watching him, expecting success. This pressure may have been the catalyst that Doolittle needed to shed his youthful rashness while developing a lush coat of logic, rationality, and responsibility. In addition to the institutional pressures, he was now father to two infant boys. Joyriding and mischief in the air, while still tempting for Jimmy, were replaced by calculation and experimentation—most of the time.

Doolittle made practice flights from Texas to California. During these, he made detailed notes on engine performance and fuel consumption. He flew from Texas to Florida to study the prominent landmarks along that route—there were not many. He took his DH-4B to McCook Field in Dayton, Ohio, the home of Air Service engineering. There significant modifications were made to his plane. A 240-gallon fuel tank and a 24-gallon oil tank were added in place of the seat in the front cockpit. Fuselage modifications were made to accommodate the new fuel configuration, also adding a slight camber to the upper wing and streamlining the bottom of the plane from the radiator cowling all the way to the tail. The wings were strengthened with additional selected spruce support ribs, tighter stitching, and four coats of dope and one of varnish. This process served to strengthen the wings—make them nearly rigid—thereby maintaining their aerodynamic efficiency to a greater degree than unmodified DH-4 wings. A turn-and-bank indicator, used to help stay in level flight under instrument conditions, was added to the rear cockpit. Old DH-4A landing gear was substituted for the B-model gear. The older gear, made of strong ash, also added four inches of ground clearance for the new Martin propeller. Wheel fairings were modified to minimize parasite drag, a monumental problem until the advent of retractable landing gear. The tailskid was reinforced to support the increased takeoff weight. Engine tests revealed that the motor burned 19.1 gallons of fuel and one and one-third gallons of oil each hour, allowing a safe flight time of more than thirteen hours. Perhaps most significant of all the modifications was the installation of a pilot relief tube.[4] Flights of such duration presented new personal, as well as technical problems. After these modifications were completed, Doolittle headed to Jacksonville, Florida.

The *Air Service News Letter*, published to inform its members and the general public about ongoing activities, described Doolittle's first attempt at the historic flight:

> Just when everything looked rosy for his successful trip across the continent from Jacksonville, Florida, to Rockwell Field, San Diego, California, a most unfortunate and unavoidable accident prevented Lieut. James H. Doolittle accomplishing his cherished ambition. While attempting to take off from Pablo Beach Sunday evening, he encountered a soft spot in the sand, occasioned by an unusually high tide and, inasmuch as his ship with its extra equipment was unusually heavy, he was thrown into a *cheval de bois* (involuntary sharp turn on the ground) breaking the propeller and left wing of his plane. . . . Although bitterly disappointed because of this sudden anti-climax after weeks of study and hard work, Lieut. Doolittle has accepted his fate with the flyer's usual pluck and good nature . . . as this accident is no reflection upon his ability as a pilot and, under like conditions, the same accident would have happened to anyone.[5]

Embarrassed but determined, Jimmy and his mechanics repaired the DH-4B and prepared for a second attempt. Time was running out for that year, as westerly winds normally increased during the fall months. Headwinds resulted in lower ground speeds and added critical minutes to flight times. As Doolittle had calculated more than eleven hours of flying time for each leg, any significant wind would prevent his accomplishing the transcontinental mission in less than one day. Flying east to west allowed for more daylight flying time, an important consideration, as aircraft instrumentation had not yet advanced to complete reliability. He knew he had to try soon, while the winds were light, or wait until next spring.

On the evening of 4 September 1922, Doolittle made his way back to Pablo Beach, this time determined not to "ground loop" in the sand. At 9:52 P.M., the DH-4B, with two pair of dice painted under Doolittle's cockpit—seven showing on one side of the fuselage, eleven showing on the other—gradually lifted into the Florida sky. A full moon shone brightly that night, a choice made to ensure illumination of the route he had practiced during the past few months. A twenty-four-hour east-to-west flight necessarily meant that at least nine of those hours would be flown in darkness. Wisely, Doolittle elected to fly the nighttime portion of the mission first, calculating that it would be easier to remain awake at the end of the mission, chasing the sun to maintain daylight conditions.[6]

He climbed to 3,500 feet above the ground and accelerated to his cruising speed of 105 miles per hour. He dodged storms near the Texas-Louisiana border but landed safely at Kelly Field after ten hours of flying. Immediately upon his landing, his ground crew replenished all the DH-4's fluids: gasoline, oil, and water. Wires were tightened, minor leaks were repaired, and a quick breakfast was served. At 8:20 A.M., Doolittle revved his engine and headed west on the final leg of the journey. Now Doolittle was in familiar territory. He had flown the westward route many times during his border-patrol days. As long as the engine held up, he was home free.

As insurance, he had coordinated for planes from Rockwell Field to join up with his modified DH-4B as he approached California to keep a close eye on his condition and occupy his mind in an effort to avoid in-flight fatigue. Doolittle landed safely at Rockwell Field eleven hours and fifteen minutes after his takeoff from Kelly Field. The flight covered 2,275 miles. His flying time was twenty-one hours and nineteen minutes, while total time for the transcontinental flight, including the refueling stop in San Antonio, was twenty-two hours and thirty minutes. The *Air Service News Letter* trumpeted the record-setting flight as "easily the biggest event in Aviation in this section of the country and perhaps the United States."[7]

Doolittle had succeeded, but more important than the flight itself was what he had learned from his efforts to achieve such a goal. From his first failure he learned that publicity prior to such attempts was a formula for humiliation. From his test flights he learned that practical data provided information needed to calculate necessary fuel, navigation, and piloting requirements. From the engineers at McCook Field and San Antonio, he began to understand the science behind flight and the limits of the technology that existed at that time. From detailed planning, he recognized the importance of logistics and ground support for long-range flights—one small step toward the development of a system of cross-country support facilities. Doolittle's achievement was more than a significant first: It was the beginning of his metamorphosis from an impulsive, sometimes unfocused pilot to a mature, conscientious aviator.

Doolittle received congratulatory messages from many of his comrades and commanders, but the most highly regarded one came from Billy Mitchell. In a tradition that has been slow to change, Doolittle received a Distinguished Flying Cross for his transcontinental flight many years after the achievement, in 1929. New assignments, however, came in a much more timely fashion. While Jimmy was resting at Rockwell after the flight, he received orders to proceed to the Air Service Engineering School at McCook Field for a new assignment as a flight-test engineer—a job he considered a high honor.

"McCook was piloting heaven," Doolittle claimed, "because there were so many different types of planes to fly and so much interesting experimental work was going on all the time. . . . As far as I was concerned, there was no better place in the world to be than McCook at that time."[8] He flew dozens of aircraft, both foreign and domestic models. He practiced flights in poor visibility by memorizing ground landmarks that allowed him to remain oriented. He participated in high-altitude flights that explored the limits of piloting without a direct oxygen supply.

In one near calamitous flight in an open-cockpit LePare, he and another test pilot had climbed to a remarkable 38,000 feet before they unknowingly drained the aircraft's oxygen supply to zero. Both suffering from hypoxia, a condition caused by insufficient oxygen supply to the brain and the body, they fell unconscious. The plane slowly descended, and when it reached approximately 20,000 feet, the duo regained their senses and recovered the aircraft to a safe landing. Doolittle's partner on that mission, Lt. Albert Stevens, had taken aerial photos to calibrate high-altitude cameras. The photos "Steve" Stevens took that day were the highest ever taken in an airplane at that time. Fortunately, they lived to tell the story.[9]

Jimmy continued to perform at air shows throughout the region. He flew solo and also with two "welded wingmen"—a wedge formation of three with one airplane close to each of the leaders wings. Doolittle described his flying like this: "Stunting was our avocation; testing was our vocation."[10]

There existed another, less glamorous side of the engineering school—classroom instruction. There aviators were taught critical aeronautical formulas for lift, drag, thrust, and pressure. They worked with engineers in the shops to construct wings that could lift more weight, sustain more acceleration, and produce less drag and then tested these ideas in the air. In essence, McCook Field was an academically demanding test-pilot school.

In light of the rigorous curriculum involved, Doolittle was finally awarded credit for his fourth and final year at the University of California School of Mines. The acceptance of civilian academic credit from an Air Service school was the first case in which a university accepted military credits—common practice in the modern USAF through the Air Force Institute of Technology (AFIT), located near Dayton, Ohio.

The award of a bachelor of arts degree paved the way for his acceptance into the postgraduate school at the Massachusetts Institute of Technology (MIT) in the fall of 1923. Jimmy moved to Cambridge but remained assigned to McCook Field to retain his flying skills. This allowed for the unusual opportunity to study aeronautics in the classroom and then test academic hypotheses in the air. After several months of academics, Doolittle selected a topic for his thesis. He planned to study accelerations, or G forces, and their impact on aircraft and pilots in flight.

After more than a hundred flight hours in a Fokker PW-7, he terminated his research after nearly ripping the wings completely off of the aircraft. Doolittle concluded that the increased pressure altered the mechanical components of force exerted upon the wing. These changing forces determine where and when the wing might suffer catastrophic failure. He concluded that the manufacturer's design limits were quite close to actual failure acceleration tolerances, but further experimentation had to be canceled after the failure of the Fokker's wings.

More important, Doolittle determined the basic rules for effects of Gs on pilots and that short-duration acceleration had less effect than sustained acceleration. He also determined that sustained G forces resulted in physical impairment and noticed that higher blood pressure in pilots meant they could sustain high-G acceleration for a longer time. This was such important work that Doolittle was awarded his master's degree in 1924 and another Distinguished Flying Cross, but not until 1929.[11] These documented discoveries are today a distinct element of basic military-pilot training and critical in piloting modern high-performance military aircraft.

Since the Army had agreed to two years of academic time at MIT, Doolittle simply continued the search for a dissertation topic. Doolittle liked school and saw an opportunity to "make some lasting contribution to aeronautics through research."[12] He decided to attack a particularly disputed subject among experienced pilots—the effects of wind on airplane performance.

After many trial flights, Doolittle determined that wind affected ground speed and thereby impacted climb gradients. But his professors rejected what appeared to be only supposition. They required support with mathematical calculations. He used formulas from the famous Ludwig Prandtl, professor of mechanics from the University of Göttingen, Germany. He took photographic data of time and distance during flight testing and measured as many variables as possible.

Doolittle's research, in short, described the impact of wind on ground speed of aircraft. This is still a fundamental concept learned by all modern pilots in basic flight school. After including the appropriate arithmetic calculations in his report, Doolittle was awarded a doctor of science degree in June 1925.[13]

Formal academics behind him, Doolittle set out to use the knowledge he had gained during his studies of aeronautical science. But first he needed a break from the meticulous, repetitious details of data collection. Doolittle and Lt. Cyrus Bettis were selected as the pilots for two major races held in 1925—the Pulitzer and the Schneider Cup. They would fly the Air Services' only R3C aircraft. Fitted with a 610-horsepower Curtiss V-1400 engine, the plane was one of the fastest ever built and was adaptable to fly with either wheels or floats. Bettis was the primary pilot for the Pulitzer and Doolittle was selected to fly the Schneider, a seaplane-only race. Cy Bettis won the Pulitzer on October 12, 1925, by seven miles per hour over the second-place finisher, Navy Lt. Alford J. Williams, also flying an R3C.

Jimmy had never flown a seaplane before. In the heat of a Washington, D.C., summer, Doolittle spent a few weeks at the Anacostia Naval Air Station learning the skills required to launch and land waterborne craft. These new skills were not only necessary to safely operate a seaplane; they were also an integral, scored part of the competition. He took to it like a young waterfowl and soon was as good at water takeoff and taxi operations as any other pilot. His race was scheduled for the end of October.

The Jacques Schneider Cup race was held near Baltimore, Maryland, on 26 October 1925. Being near Washington, D.C., several high-ranking military personalities were in attendance. Representing the Air Service was its chief, Maj. Gen. Mason Patrick. His equivalent from the Navy, R. Adm. William A. Moffet, could not attend, but he sent his wife in his place. Several aircraft-company presidents and their representatives were there, and the famed pioneer naval aviator and Wright flying student in 1911, Commander John Rogers, also made an appearance. Perhaps most important, Orville Wright was there. This was a very high-profile race.

Five took to the air; only three finished. Doolittle, flying the same R3C that Bettis had flown, now fitted with pontoons, won. His margin of victory was greater than thirty miles per hour faster than the second-place finisher. Had Navy Lieutenant Cuddihy completed the course, the margin would have been only ten miles per hour, but his engine caught fire on the last lap and he was forced to retire. Doolittle executed a grand wifferdill—rapidly climbing to exchange airspeed for altitude—after completing the course, then a perfect landing. He was towed to the pier, where he received a tremendous ovation from the crowd. General Patrick was beaming, and Joe was beaming too. The naval contingent was not.[14]

Not only did Doolittle win the Schneider Cup race that year; he and Bettis also received the Mackay Trophy for the most meritorious military flights of the year. As testimony to the remarkable development in aircraft technology, Doolittle's average lap speed was an "astonishing" 232.573 miles per hour. What made the feat so remarkable was how far ahead of the previous years' winning times he flew. The winning time in 1924 was an average of 167.083 miles per hour. Doolittle surpassed the time by 65.49 miles per hour; "astonishing" was an appropriate word.[15] It was events such as this one, in which an Air Service pilot handily won a seaplane-only race, that fueled the rivalry begun when Billy Mitchell predicted the death of the battleship in 1921.

It would be less than a year before Mitchell himself was sunk. His court martial, resulting in a conviction for insubordination, was one of the most famous events in American military history. He was both a hero and a stubborn fool to those young airmen who admired his views and believed in the efficacy of airpower. Jimmy was pragmatic, not emotional, about the Mitchell affair. Mitchell "became a zealot," Doolittle wrote, "and like all zealots, he eventually lost sight of the objective."[16]

When the Doolittles returned to McCook Field, Jimmy found himself in a new job—chief of the Flight Test Section. He was a natural choice. Jimmy had academic credentials, experience in many aircraft, and fearlessness in the air. He flew whatever he wanted, whenever he wanted, and participated in the engineering and science behind new testing. Much of the progress in design came only after trial and error in the air. Doolittle loved that challenge.

One of those who had witnessed the Schneider Cup race was C. M. Keyes, president of the Curtiss-Wright aircraft company. In early 1926, Keyes convinced the Air Service to allow Jimmy to demonstrate the capabilities of the Curtiss P-1 Hawk fighter plane outfitted with a Curtiss D-12 engine. Their destination was South America. Jimmy was released for several months without pay. Curtiss picked up the tab for his military salary and then some. The only drawback to the duty was that Joe and the boys had to stay in Ohio. That spring, Doolittle packed up and headed for Santiago, Chile, by ship.

The Chilean flyers were eager to welcome the Schneider Cup winner in style. On 23 May 1926, they hosted a cocktail party for the arriving delegation. The drink of the evening was a Peruvian brandy mixed with lemon and sugar called a pisco sour. A few drinks led to boasting, boasting led to demonstrations of physical prowess, and these demonstrations led to disaster for Jimmy. While he was trying to execute a difficult balancing trick while hanging over a second-story ledge, his handhold gave way and he plummeted to the ground, feet first. The result was two broken ankles.[17]

Once again, humiliated in front of his peers, Doolittle could only think what Joe would have said to him after his childish demonstration. He was being paid to provide a service to the Curtiss company, and now that income was in jeopardy. According to Jimmy, she would have simply picked up a spoon and "put it to one eye as if viewing me under a microscope, and stared at me without saying a word."[18] She would not have approved. He would not be denied. After having both legs set in casts, Doolittle began his demonstration season by having his engineer rig clasps that held his fresh casts to the rudder pedals.

"The cast on my right foot broke when I did a snap roll to the right," Jimmy remembered. "Then the cast broke on the left foot, so I had two broken casts on two broken legs, and that was quite uncomfortable." The casts were reinforced, and metal corset stays were added to the contraption so that Jimmy had complete use of his feet, albeit impaired by the casts.[19]

Doolittle flew demonstrations in Bolivia and Argentina, where Curtiss sold several Hawks. Jimmy, suffering from ankle pain caused by improper casting, returned to McCook and his old job in the renamed Army Air Corps and immediately requested sick leave. By 5 October, Doolittle had been admitted to Walter Reed General Hospital. Joe and the boys moved temporarily from McCook to Washington, D.C. Jimmy needed them near the hospital while he endured physical therapy to strengthen his now mending ankles. It was quite a price to pay for showing off while under the influence of a few pisco sours. He was not returned to flying status until 5 April 1927.

Recuperating at Walter Reed gave Doolittle time to think. His mind was never idle as far as flying was concerned. Almost immediately after his return to McCook Field, he began practicing to accomplish an aerial maneuver thought impossible by most pilots: the outside loop. This maneuver is flown with the pilot riding on the outside of the path carved in the sky, all the while experiencing negative G forces pushing the blood in the body toward the head. A normal loop, by comparison, is flown as if riding a roller coaster that accelerates downward and climbs up and over, placing the rider upside down but on the inside of the maneuver and under positive G forces that push toward the seat of the machine, not the head.

Flying the P-1 Hawk, Doolittle began practicing the first half of the maneuver by climbing to a safe altitude and pushing the control stick forward. This pitched the aircraft nose-first toward the ground. He continued to push until the plane began to tuck under the vertical position, negative G forces climbing and forcing him against his seat restraints as if to throw him from the cockpit. He tried this several times.

The performance of the outside loop for the first time was almost an accident. I pushed this airplane over into a dive and then pushed it under a little ways and I began to feel the inverted load and my weight against the safety belt. It seemed to be alright [*sic*], felt pretty good, and so I pushed a little further and the first thing I knew, to my amazement, I was upright, and I couldn't wait to get down and land.[20]

Lt. James T. Hutchinson, one of Jimmy's friends, witnessed the outside loop on one of Jimmy's subsequent flights. Then Doolittle gathered the rest of the test pilots and performed the maneuver, which was immediately reported in the local newspaper. Doolittle's headline came less than a week after Charles "Slim" Lindbergh had successfully crossed the Atlantic Ocean alone in the specially modified Ryan NYP *Spirit of St. Louis*. Slim's arrival in Paris made headlines worldwide. Doolittle's outside loop did not receive such publicity.

After another season of air shows and testing, under the same type of agreement made between Curtiss-Wright and the Air Corps in 1926, Doolittle headed to South America for another demonstration tour in Peru, Bolivia, Chile, Uruguay, and Argentina.

This trip to South America began far better than the first. Jimmy flew demonstrations in many towns, soared above the Andes and the Amazon, and transported supplies to remote gold mines to show the utility of aircraft. His flying must have impressed the Bolivian government, for he was awarded that nation's highest honor for a foreigner: the National Order of the Condor.[21]

Then in Chile, a visiting British pilot convinced Doolittle to take him up for a test ride in a Curtiss P-1 floatplane. Jimmy did not recognize his passenger's lack of skill in time, and the floatplane nosed under during the takeoff and both men narrowly escaped with their lives. The airplane sank. Shades of the rogue youngster had surfaced but were quickly controlled during the remainder of the demonstration tour. When Doolittle returned to the United States in 1926, his future military career was uncertain.

Chapter 3

Landing Blind

W HILE JIMMY DOOLITTLE had been dazzling the South Americans, the Guggenheim fund, established by philanthropist Daniel Guggenheim, assisted by his son Harry, had taken up researching the problems involved with flying through clouds. The function of the Guggenheim fund was to serve as "a spark plug" that stimulated interest in the problem under investigation and then transferred the investigation to a different agency of industry.[1] Beginning in the fall of 1926, ideas about fog dissipation devices, instrumentation that could help pilots remain oriented in zero visibility, and aids to precision navigation were being discussed. The turn and bank indicator, developed by Elmer Sperry during World War I, was still the primary instrument in the cockpit—when instruments were used at all.

The problem with flying in poor weather was that a loss of visual reference to a known horizon forced the pilot to rely upon some other means to determine where the horizon might be. An instrument that reflected an artificial horizon inside the cockpit did not exist. When a pilot entered fog or a cloud, physiology took over in place of visual cues in determining the orientation of the airplane. Flying by the "seat of the pants," as it was frequently called, did not work for extended durations in bad weather. Disorientation resulted as the pilot's body reacted to secondary, and often false, sensory inputs rather than the primary visual cues provided by maintaining contact with a known horizon outside the airplane. Despite the introduction of the Barony Chair, a spinning chair that introduced young pilots to the unusual effects of shifts in the orientation of the inner ear to sustained motion, there was no concrete method to fight disorientation except to remain clear of all bad weather at all times.[2] Modern pilots understand these concepts, but the science of aerospace physiology remained largely unexplored in the 1920s. Aside from the external forces acting upon a pilot, technological advances were sought to assist the pilot in overcoming human shortcomings.

Directional radio beacon development was proceeding at McCook Field but was not emphasized by other agencies, like the Bureau of Standards, until 1926. Until that time, direction finding had been predicated upon audio signals interpreted by the pilot to home to a known radio transmitter. After the Bureau of Standards Aeronautical Research Division got involved, a visual system was invented that consisted of vibrating, parallel white reeds that showed which way the plane had drifted off course.

Despite such advances, a device capable of transmitting glide path information to the pilot had not been developed. For this reason, many scientists remained skeptical about the possibilities of accomplishing "blind landings." With practice, pilots became fairly proficient in flying through clouds using instrumentation then available—primarily, the Sperry turn and bank indicator. Landing blind, however, was another matter altogether.

In August 1928, Harry F. Guggenheim announced that funding was being made available to open a Full Flight Laboratory for the purpose of studying flight in poor weather conditions. The Guggenheims had requested the use of a skilled pilot to act as the director of their newest attempt to consider "fundamental aeronautical and aerodynamical [sic] problems." Five flyers, both

Army and Navy, were nominated, and Doolittle was selected. The vice president of the Guggenheim fund, Capt. Emory S. Land, an officer in the Construction Corps of the Navy, had selected Doolittle because of "not only a lifetime of flying, but a technical education that has given him a distinct advantage in the development of new equipment."[3] No other pilot could boast such credentials.

By late fall, the funds had been allocated and two aircraft were purchased to support the program. A Vought O2U-1 Corsair served as the cross-country platform and was not equipped for blind landings. It was accepted on 21 November 1928, and the first passenger who flew in it was Harry Guggenheim. A Consolidated NY-2 Husky was converted into the blind-flying test aircraft. The Husky spent much time being modified in the Radio Frequency Laboratories in Boonton, New Jersey.

During November and December, Jimmy flew many flights with passengers to gain experience in the aircraft. Among those were his wife, Joe, and his young boys—both of whom later went on to fly as pilots for the U.S. Air Force.[4] A removable canvas hood was added to the Husky's rear cockpit so that the pilot could not see outside. The front cockpit remained open for a safety observer who had access to the flight controls. Lt. Ben Kelsey filled that position. "From the start," Doolittle wrote, Kelsey "was a full-fledged member of the team and did much of the experimental work. His piloting help, criticisms of the test carried out, and sound technical counsel contributed greatly to the results achieved."[5]

In fact, the entire operation that the Guggenheims established at Mitchel Field, Long Island, New York, was decidedly a team effort. The Fund provided the money, the Army provided the aircrew (Doolittle and Kelsey) and mechanic (Jack Dalton), the Navy provided the vice president and administrator of the fund (Capt. "Jerry" Land), the Bureau of Standards and Sperry resolved problems associated with inaccurate instrumentation, and MIT sent Professor William G. Brown to assist in the direction of the research program. The result was the right people assembled at the right place and the right time attacking a problem that had been considered impossible by pilots and scientists alike.

As the Wright brothers had solved the basic problem of aircraft control by 1903, the Full Flight team had two major problems that had to be resolved before blind landing could be attempted. First, an accurate altitude-measuring device was needed so that the pilot would know, within five feet, when he was about to touch down. Second, an accurate turn and heading indicator was essential so that the pilot could line up the aircraft on a suitable landing field without actually seeing one in front of his aircraft. For the altimeter design, Doolittle turned to two German-born brothers, Paul and Otto Kollsman, who had organized an instrument-manufacturing company in 1928. For the other problem, he turned to Elmer Sperry. With the help of his son, Elmer Jr., and Preston Basset, another Sperry employee, the engineering genius set out to provide a solution to Doolittle's problems.

While the technicians studied the instrument problem, Jimmy gathered all the information from previous weather-flying programs that he could find. Physical modifications to aircraft in attempts to better sense when the ground was approaching were deemed too intrusive to the critical nature of the landing and, therefore, impractical.[6] Essentially, the Guggenheim team had to begin from scratch. The chosen method centered on the development of new, highly accurate flight performance instruments.

The result of their efforts was the invention of three new instruments. Kollsman's detailed craftsmanship and near-watchmaker precision resulted in the construction of an altimeter that was accurate to a known elevation plus or minus five feet. This improvement was ten times more accurate than anything then used in an aircraft. The Sperry team devised a gyro-driven artificial horizon that displayed the aircraft bank relative to the surface of the earth and a directional gyrocompass that was set to a known heading and then maintained that heading without magnetic input but, rather, by the spinning of a gyroscope. The development of these three instruments paved the way for Doolittle's ability to take off, fly, and land without reference to the ground.

The new instruments, the turn and bank indicator, and a suite of radio-navigation equipment filled the rear cockpit of the NY-2. The Corsair, on the other hand, was not so fully equipped. That deficiency almost cost Doolittle his life before he could demonstrate blind landings for the Guggenheims. In March, Doolittle began a routine hop from Buffalo to Mitchel Field after a technical meeting. As he approached the east coast of New York, the weather began to deteriorate. Jimmy desperately looked for a suitable landing field, but low clouds had rolled in and covered the area. Running low on fuel, Doolittle saw what he believed to be an airfield's light beacon and decided to make a landing approach. Into the soup he flew with his landing light blazing, hoping to break out of the clouds over a wide-open landing field. Instead he snagged the top of a tree, tearing the fabric on one of the wings, barely maintaining control; he circled and found enough space to put the Corsair down but struck another tree with the left wing before coming to a violent halt, hanging nearly upside down in his safety belt. Miraculously, he sustained no injuries.[7]

In years past, such an event might have been more Jimmy's own doing, more an indication of irresponsibility in the air—but not this time. Weather was the single greatest variable in the air. Unexpected storms, evening fog, and gusty winds associated with passing cold fronts all occurred as they do today, but no accurate weather forecasting was available. Even highly experienced aviators did not have the cockpit tools that could rescue them from flying in limited-visibility weather, either in clouds or during the darkness of night. That night Jimmy relearned one of the most important rules for a pilot: "Learn your limitations, gradually expand them, but never go beyond them."[8]

After that narrow escape, Doolittle began to practice flying the Husky. He had to; it was the only thing left to fly. Through the summer months he flew hundreds of practice flights in the backseat. By September he felt prepared to test his ability to accomplish a blind landing in poor weather. The NY-2 was packed with instruments: normal engine instruments, magnetic compass, turn and bank indicator, earth inductor compass, directional gyro, artificial horizon, airspeed indicator, altimeter, rate of climb indicator, outside-air thermometer, vibrating-reed homing-range indicator, and vibrating-reed marker-beacon indicator. "Considerable thought was given," Doolittle wrote, "to the location or arrangement of each instrument to facilitate reading and reduce pilot fatigue."[9]

On the morning of 24 September, thick fog coated the Mitchel Field landing zone. Doolittle hopped in the NY-2 alone after having the beacons turned on and climbed into the fog. Joe, Elmer Sperry Jr., and Dalton waited for his reappearance from the east side of the field. He landed successfully. But this was only a warm-up, because Harry Guggenheim had not yet arrived from his nearby residence; the fog was too dense to drive quickly.

Doolittle was confident in what was about to happen. Guggenheim arrived, and after a brief discussion it was decided that Doolittle would fly while covered by the hood and Kelsey would sit in the front seat as a safety pilot and observer. The fog was still thick but had lifted so that the ground was becoming visible from the air. The restriction to his sight was absolutely essential to prove beyond doubt the accomplishment of Guggenheim's team.

Ben Kelsey placed his arms visibly on the outside of his cockpit, demonstrating that he was not in control of the airplane. Doolittle lined up for takeoff using his localizer-reed device, and off they went. He climbed straight ahead to 1,000 feet above the ground. After reaching that altitude, he turned 180 degrees to the left and pointed the plane back toward the airfield, just a little bit south of the landing zone. After passing the field, he initiated his final turn to the left and intercepted the radio guidance "beam." He began his descent to 200 feet and waited until the vibrating reeds quit moving, indicating he was over the final-descent point.

There was no device that told Jimmy if he was flying a proper glide angle for landing. A useable glide-path indicator would not be invented until a few years later. To accomplish a controlled landing from a known point, Doolittle had perfected a method for flying a known path by maintaining a known airspeed and correcting slightly for the direction of the surface winds. His dissertation had exposed him to the knowledge of winds that he required to compute and execute this final landing approach. He set his power to maintain sixty miles per hour in a slight descent until he flew the aircraft to the ground. The strengthened struts absorbed the blow (about twelve feet per second) and, on most landings, resulted in a relatively smooth touchdown. A mark placed next to his throttle assured the proper power setting for the descent. On this historic attempt, however, he misjudged his descent rate and hit with enough force to bounce back into the air once and then land for good. "Despite previous practice," he recalled, "the final approach and landing were sloppy."[10] Sloppy or not, the feat had been accomplished.

The team members were rightfully proud of their achievement. Lieutenant Kelsey later wrote that "the demonstration was perhaps the most significant development since the original Wright brothers' flight."[11] Harry Guggenheim placed the accomplishment in a more practical perspective:

> It is significant that the achievement is realized through the aid of only three instruments which are not already the standard equipment of an airplane. In other words, with the commercial manufacture of these instruments, the necessary equipment for fog flying will be neither expensive nor complicated, but of such a nature that it is readily available to the average pilot, and easily comprehended. The commercial practicability of the development is, therefore, assured from the start.[12]

Doolittle's pride ran deep. For the rest of his life he believed that "assisting in the instrumentation necessary to do the flight was my greatest contribution to aviation."[13] The fact that Doolittle later held this achievement above his aerial demonstration and racing accomplishments, above his still-to-come pioneering work with Shell Petroleum, even above his successful execution of the Tokyo Raid in 1942, and his command experiences in WWII is a clear indication that he understood the significance of this first-ever blind landing. From that day forward, every aircraft equipped with the capability to fly in limited visibility was afforded the instrumentation needed because of the success of the Doolittle-led Guggenheim Full Flight Laboratory's quest to solve the problems associated with blind flying and landing. "Flying by instruments soon outgrew the early experimental phase. It became a practical reality, and aviation entered a new era."[14]

Blind flying would soon be taught to all Army Air Corps pilots before they received their wings and, today, accounts for over one third of the curriculum at undergraduate pilot training. In the broadest sense, Doolittle was absolutely right. He and his team had applied science to modify technology in a successful effort to solve a practical problem. Jimmy Doolittle earned his wizard's hat that day.

Their mission accomplished, the Guggenheims closed the Full Flight Laboratory at Mitchel Field. The military services and the Bureau of Standards were left to pick up the research where Doolittle and the lab had left off. Jimmy once again had a decision to make, his time on loan now over—to remain in the Army or to find employment in the civilian sector. His boys were in elementary school, and he did not much care for uprooting them as frequently as a military career often required. Joe's and Jimmy's mothers were both in ill health, and his obligations to them were increasing. He was presented an offer from Shell Petroleum that, under his present family circumstances, he simply could not refuse—a salary three times his military pay.[15]

Chapter 4

Fast Flying and Fuel

L IEUTENANT DOOLITTLE was now Dr. Doolittle. His paycheck had tripled, his family was happy and would soon be settled in St. Louis, and he continued flying. The Shell Company had hired Jimmy at a time when all the major oil companies were hiring celebrity aviators. Texaco had hired Frank Hawkes, Standard Oil had Eddie Aldrin, Al Williams was at Gulf, and Roscoe Turner ended up at Gilmore Oil. Doolittle's job was to act as a Shell product representative on the race circuit and otherwise provide positive press coverage for the company. Soon Jimmy was coordinating the aviation-related activity at all three Shell locations: St. Louis, New York, and San Francisco.

As an added perk, Shell had purchased a spanking-new Lockheed Vega to the tune of $25,000 and made it available for Doolittle's use. He promptly crashed it into a snowbank. The Doolittles, all of them, had piled their luggage and personal effects into the Vega for the flight to St. Louis from Mitchel Field. The airplane was overloaded and would not lift off. Good fortune prevented the plane from going up in a ball of fire when the fuel tank ruptured after the landing gear collapsed as Jimmy tried to muscle the plane into the cold, snowy February air. His embarrassment was complete when a major New York newspaper ran the headline "Ex-Army Pilot Crashes in Snow Before Start."[1] It was an uncomfortable beginning for such a high-paying civilian job.

By the spring of 1930, Doolittle and an aerial demonstration team sponsored by Shell were touring Europe. Joe stayed in the new residence in St. Louis. The European tour went smoothly until it reached Hungarian soil. Perhaps because Jimmy had escaped Joe's watchful eye, or maybe because he had been challenged to do it, he successfully accomplished a dangerous stunt in his Curtiss Hawk aircraft. He flew under one of the low Danube River bridges while his challenger and a small crowd watched him—and he did it at night.[2] The flying team returned to the States in July. The rest of that summer was an unhappy time as Jimmy's mother took a turn for the worse and died on 22 September.

Having a little extra money, Doolittle bought his own plane with the intention of making it one of the fastest in the world. A Shell-owned Beech Travel-Air had crashed, and Jimmy bought the remains for his project. After adding a powerful Pratt & Whitney engine and some aerodynamic modifications, the *Doolittle 400* was ready for flight. That flying exhibition nearly resulted in Doolittle's death. It was his closest call ever.

After a brief display of the aircraft's speed, Jimmy tested the 400's strength with a high-speed pull-up. The G forces were too great. The ailerons were ripped from their stations and the aircraft became uncontrollable. Doolittle barely had time to jump, pull his parachute rip cord, and wait for the chute to inflate before he smacked the ground—unbelievably, uninjured.[3] The plane, and the investment, were a total loss.

Undeterred, Jimmy sought an aircraft to enter in the 1931 Bendix cross-country air race. After a conversation with E. M. "Matty" Laird, Jimmy landed a ride—the Laird Super Solution. The winner of the race, from Burbank, California, to Cleveland, Ohio, would pocket $7,500 and another $2,500 if that pilot could continue on to the east coast, breaking the west-east transcontinental record, as well.

Seven other pilots gathered at United Airport in Burbank for the race, including a young Army captain, Ira C. Eaker, who had expanded upon Doolittle's instrument-flying work by once soaring coast-to-coast under an instrument hood. The flyers departed in short intervals after midnight on 4 September 1931, Jimmy taking off at 1:40 A.M. After two stops and accumulating an elapsed time of nine hours, ten minutes, and twenty-one seconds, Doolittle landed in Cleveland. Although uncertain of his Bendix victory, he had no time to waste if the west-east record was to fall as he had planned. Through marginal weather conditions, he successfully pressed on to Newark with a new record and prize money for the effort. The old transcontinental record had been shattered by more than an hour. Doolittle's time was eleven hours and eleven minutes. Inspired by the fact that Joe and the boys were waiting in Cleveland, he refueled and turned right around for Cleveland, where he arrived later that evening.

There, a tired, happy, and somewhat wealthier Doolittle was reunited with his family. He now held the distinction of being the first pilot to cross America in less than one day and the first to cross in less than half a day. By winning the Bendix race and setting the west-east transcontinental record, Doolittle was demonstrating the practicality of air travel. Coast-to-coast travel in less than twelve hours was appealing to many as a time-saver and a business advantage. The increased reliability and passenger capacity of aircraft was becoming a reality, one that would spur the growth of the commercial airline industry in America. To emphasize this point, he hopped into his plane and flew back to St. Louis that same night!

Barely recovered from the Bendix race, Doolittle and the Super Solution entered the Thompson race on 7 September. The Super Solution was not a maneuverable pylon racer. Despite attempts to modify its performance, it seemed continually misrigged and unstable in the tight pylon turns at high speeds. Doolittle blew a piston near the end of the race and did not finish. A stubby Gee Bee Z won with an average speed approaching 240 miles per hour.

After his disappointment at the 1931 Thompson race, Jimmy continued showing the Shell Petroleum Company colors across the nation. He flew several different aircraft, all of them emblazoned with the red Shell logo, from coast to coast. In one publicity campaign, he retraced the significant locations that highlighted George Washington's life. Well publicized by the Shell team, the bicentennial of Washington's birth offered a patriotic theme to a country that had been ripped apart by the collapse of the American economy in 1929. On that occasion, Doolittle flew a Shell-yellow Lockheed Orion 9C Special named *Shellightning*. The 24–25 July flight covered fourteen eastern states and more than 2,600 miles. The flight also celebrated the 157th anniversary of the postal service, founded by Benjamin Franklin. Overall, it was a great success for Shell, the postal service, and Doolittle. There were no trophies awarded, just company gratitude.

Once again, the racing season was rapidly approaching and Doolittle was looking for a solid entry into the competition. His choice was a Laird Super Solution modified with retractable landing gear. By eliminating the drag resulting from an extended undercarriage, Doolittle figured that he could add more than fifty miles per hour to his race speed. The initial test flight supported his claims, but a failure in the landing-gear lowering system could not be rectified in flight. Doolittle bellied in, damaging the aircraft so badly that there was no hope of repairs before the race, less than two weeks away.

Finding another aircraft was not difficult. Many companies sought Doolittle's reputation and skills. In this case, an R-1 of Granville's design was made available. The red-and-white Gee Bee was nothing but power and fuel. Under its cowling roared a 750-horsepower Wasp engine, one of the most powerful built at the time. Even Doolittle approached the craft with deliberation. It was only eighteen feet long. Carrying such a huge engine and being so stubby, the craft tended toward instability. As Doolittle discovered, the plane could not be flown without holding the control stick. The design actually placed the Gee Bee in a category reserved today for modern fly-by-wire fighters—it was statically unstable in flight. Doolittle wrote, "I didn't trust this little monster."[4] He was right in his caution. Gee Bees had been involved in several fatal crashes, including one that took the life of its designer. It had earned its reputation as not only the fastest but also the most dangerous aircraft flown at that time.

Jimmy qualified fastest in the field for the Thompson and went on to win the hundred-mile race with a record speed of 252.686 miles per hour. This speed was far below what the plane was capable of achieving. Jimmy had qualified at nearly 300 miles per hour only a few days before. Joe and the boys were at the race, however, so Jimmy flew cautiously enough to increase his safety margin but fast enough to win the race. Joe's influence was clearly the driving force behind Jimmy's retirement from racing shortly thereafter.

Racing served many purposes, whether in automobiles or aircraft. Technological developments continually pushed cars and planes to faster speeds. The fundamentals of that development found application in commercial ventures to improve these vehicles. Daring drivers and pilots thrilled crowds but often paid the ultimate price for their adventurous spirits. Doolittle, having escaped literally dozens of these catastrophes, finally concluded that the risks involved in racing outweighed the rewards of earning championships. No one was more relieved than Joe. This was not to say that Doolittle had given up taking risks, for he certainly had not. Those risks yet to be taken were found in business and in war, no longer around the race course.

It was about this time that commercial-airline fuel consumption surpassed that of private planes in America for the first time. By the 1950s, airline companies would buy nearly two thirds of all aviation fuel sold. Reliable planes like the Douglas DC-2 and DC-3 sustained the airlines' growth in the late 1930s. In this rapidly expanding industry, there were sales to be made. Shell Oil wanted a big piece of the action.

Jimmy Doolittle realized that all facets of aviation technology were undergoing rapid development, particularly engines. Larger, more powerful motors were guzzling aviation fuel by the millions of gallons. But fuel development had stagnated. Interestingly, there was a general understanding among pilots that West Coast gasoline provided better engine performance and more race victories. In fact, California gas was usually imported for racing planes. The high concentration of certain elements seemed to preserve pistons during races. Clearly, research was needed to find out why.

Because of his continuing association with the Army Air Corps as a reserve major, Doolittle was aware of new military planes in development that would require fuel of superior quality. High octane ratings, approaching 100, were anticipated for these aircraft engines, which did not yet exist. Military planes in those days used a variety of fuels that ranged from 65 to 87 octane. Doolittle convinced his bosses that the research needed to develop 100-octane fuel would be an important investment in the future of the company.

> I believed that there was a future for 100-octane fuel, but there were no engines to use it, and it was like the hen and the egg, which came first? If you waited for engines to be developed for 100-octane fuel, they'd never be developed, because there'd be no fuel for them. So I felt that we had to go ahead . . . and make the fuel available. And when the fuel was available at a reasonable price, I felt that there would be enough engines developed . . . that it would be a profitable venture. This turned out to be true, but it was a gamble.[5]

During these years of economic turmoil, this idea was a hard sell. Ironically, Doolittle found that his academic credentials, not his pilot skills, made the greatest difference in convincing skeptics of the potential of 100-octane fuel. Jimmy believed that to sell technical ideas to technical people, the salesman needed excellent technical credentials. An MIT doctor of science degree was the ticket that gained him audience with the scientists who made company decisions. "I think there are two great advantages to an advanced degree," Doolittle said. "One is the increased knowledge and greater capability that you have, and the other is the prestige it gives you with your associates—particularly those who have advanced degrees."[6]

By 1934, Shell had produced its first batch of 100-octane fuel for testing at Wright Field, near old McCook Field, home of Army Air Corps flight testing. The new fuel not only increased power; it saved between 10 and 20 percent on consumption. By 1938, the Air Corps was recommending 100-octane fuel for all its combat aircraft.

Hundred-octane began as a scientific curiosity by blending 70-octane with chemicals such as tetraethyl lead and hydrogen. In 1938 an alkylation process demonstrated potential for increasing production of 100-octane fuel. Cold-acid alkylation made it possible to raise 1943 production of 100-octane to 15 million gallons per day. Until that time, 100-octane was prohibitively expensive.

Fuel additives that became effective for full-power operations were used to minimize misfires. These additives resulted in the dual-octane system and became the industry norm. By mid-1940, all British fighters had been converted to operate on 100/130—the highest octane available. This fuel produced higher manifold pressures, giving every engine an effective 30 percent increase in power.

The fuels used by the air forces gave engines at least 20 percent more power, while planes developed 6 percent more speed and better climb performance than with lower-octane fuels. The Navy had also made the transition to high-octane fuels by 1938. The RAF was able, using U.S. 100-octane fuel, to get 1,700 horsepower from Merlin engines rather than the 1,000 horsepower provided on lower-octane fuel. Commercial airlines also benefited from 100-octane fuel. Using the military fuel, they were able to shorten takeoff distance and increase range. Flying became more economical.[7]

In 1933, during the early phases of research and development of this new fuel, Jimmy toured the world in his P-6 Curtiss Hawk. Joe went along this time. Wherever they went, the Shell banner followed. The trip began in the Far East—Tokyo, Kobe, Shanghai, the Dutch East Indies, Burma, India, Iraq, and Egypt—and then on to Europe. The trip served to better acquaint him with world geography, while introducing 100-octane fuel to prospective buyers, particularly the British.

The Japanese, who invaded China in 1937 initiating the Second World War, even then closely monitored Doolittle's travels.[8] More important, Doolittle witnessed the advances in aeronautics around the world—from the Kobe wind tunnels to Berlin. He determined that the United States was falling behind in aviation technology.

These fears had existed since 1934 when the Air Corps had attempted to substitute for fired airmail contractors. Failures and several fatalities were caused by outdated military equipment, mostly a lack of poor-weather-flying instrumentation, and inexperienced pilots. The embarassing two-month mail incident was clearly a case in which military zeal on the part of Air Corps leadership, particularly Maj. Gen. Benjamin D. Foulois, Chief of the Air Corps, coupled with technical shortcomings cost lives and aircraft.

As a result of the fiasco, Newton D. Baker was asked to investigate the Air Corps and provide a report. Baker had been the secretary of war during World War I. More than one hundred interviews were conducted, resulting in more than four thousand pages of testimony.[9] The board concluded that American aviation was not as bad off as many would have the nation believe and that the organization of the Air Corps as it was attached to the Army should remain unchanged. "I was disgusted at the board's conclusions," Doolittle wrote.[10] The findings were signed off upon almost unanimously—Jimmy wrote the dissenting opinion, one that Foulois later wished he had also signed.

> I am convinced that the required air force can be more rapidly organized, equipped, and trained if it is completely separated from the Army and developed as an entirely separate arm. If complete separation is not the desire of the committee, I recommend an air force as part of the Army, but with a separate budget, a separate promotion list, and removed from the control of the General Staff.[11]

When he was not busy working on a committee or traveling the globe, Jimmy continued flying in air shows across America. It is a remarkable commentary on the state of flight regulations that during the late 30s, he had been fined, grounded, and chastised by the Civil Aeronautics Authority (CAA) for flying too low, too close to people, and landing in illegal landing zones. He did not take these punishments seriously. In fact, he had forgotten all about them over time.[12]

The dichotomy of this propensity to violate flight regulations contradicted his pleas for improved flight safety and air discipline. To understand this apparent "do as I say, not as I do" attitude, one must realize that in the late 1930s, aircraft did not fill the skies as they now do. Nonetheless, it remains inexplicable that Jimmy preached strict adherence on one hand, while enjoying the delights that stunting provided on the other. It is a part of Doolittle's personality that cannot definitively be explained. Despite his undeniable piloting skills and frequent flights as a test pilot, he sometimes reverted to reckless behavior that challenged institutionally accepted rules of air discipline.

Jimmy had demonstrated a disregard for flight safety and lapses in judgment at various times during his flying career. His supreme confidence and proven piloting skills had saved him from a dozen deaths. Had he refrained from some of his less carefully deliberated aerial escapades, however, he certainly would have wrecked fewer planes. In his case, the margin between living legend and casualty statistic was a narrow one.

By 1939, after a few additional trips to Europe, Doolittle recognized that the European war would undoubtedly envelop America—it was simply a question of when. Earlier, during a 1937 trip to Germany, Jimmy had wined and dined with his aerial counterpart Ernst Udet. He had known Udet for several years from the air-show circuit. Like Doolittle, he had a "proclivity for having fun in airplanes and flying them to the edge of their performance limits."[13] It was through his friendship with Udet that Doolittle surmised the buildup of Nazi airpower in the late 1930s. His perceptions were strong enough and clear enough that he initiated contact with Maj. Gen. Henry H. "Hap" Arnold, Chief of the Army Air Corps.

Major General Arnold was already well aware that the Nazis were approaching a brink. He had become friends with European scientists of Jewish descent who had escaped rising nationalism and were working diligently in American universities on aeronautics problems. Many European travelers, Charles Lindbergh for one, had informed Arnold that the Germans were building a huge, and very advanced, air force. Doolittle's report simply added fuel to a raging fire. On 1 September 1939, the Nazis marched into Poland.

It had become clear that America would be involved in a shooting war, and Doolittle wanted to be involved. Arnold, pleased that Jimmy had volunteered to rejoin the Army Air Corps, agreed that by the summer of 1940 Doolittle would be back in a military uniform. Arnold had to bend a few regulations just to get the field-grade reserve officer back.[14]

While Jimmy waited for the Army's call, he was named president of the Institute of Aeronautical Sciences (IAS), a symbolic honor but also an opportunity to rub elbows with those most involved in developing aeronautical-science and aviation technology. In that position, he reached the pinnacle of his academic career. Doolittle would not have then believed that he had yet to reach a similar peak in his flying career—even considering his many records and victories.

By 1 July 1940, Doolittle had arrived at his first duty assignment, as the Air Corps representative at the Allison engine plant in Indianapolis. Here he put his technical expertise and business experience to good use in troubleshooting the process of transforming an automobile factory into an aircraft-engine production line.[15] Additionally, Jimmy was given a P-40 so that he could get around the production lines quickly. Because instrument flying was not allowed in pursuit-type aircraft, General Arnold issued him a personal waiver to these rules: "This authority is granted in recognition of your exceptional qualifications and to enable the Air Corps to obtain valuable information on the behavior and flying characteristics of modern pursuit-type airplanes under instrument flying conditions."[16]

Doolittle was a meticulous critic when it came to factory production. His experience at Shell was advantageous in dealing with large civilian companies. His technical training provided him the mental tools to understand what needed to be done to produce a useful product. He knew Hap Arnold well enough to know that failure would result in removal—friends or not.

As part of Jimmy's duty, Arnold sent him to England in the fall of 1941. Arnold had just returned from a trip there, on which he had been secretly introduced to the Whittle jet engine. He had not had sufficient time to evaluate factory procedure and gather ideas that American industry might be able to use in its transition to a wartime economy. Immediately upon his return, Arnold called for Doolittle, who was ordered to report on the strengths and weaknesses of the British aircraft industry. He was gone for five weeks, 7 September through 13 October.

Doolittle was welcomed in England, where his contributions to aviation technology were recognized. The petroleum secretary of Great Britain would later announce that the British would not have emerged victorious from the Battle of Britain without 100-octane fuel: "This octane was thirteen points higher than the fuel used by German aircraft. Those extra thirteen points ended the threat of any Nazi invasion of England."[17]

He did a little flying and a lot of touring. He produced a detailed report that contained 132 recommendations—an average of nearly four each day he was in England. He made observations concerning weaponry, salvage practices, training cycles, advantages of different engine types, women factory workers, administration, cockpit design—the list was extensive, detailed, yet succinct. Arnold was impressed by Doolittle's work because he understood the process. During the First World War, Arnold had done the same sort of thing, writing a similar report on American industrial effectiveness after the war had ended.[18] Doolittle was gaining Arnold's respect at a critical time in America's military buildup. Everything was being geared to meet FDR's goal of fifty thousand airplanes produced each year.[19]

After the attack on Pearl Harbor, Doolittle immediately requested a combat assignment. Instead, Arnold moved him to Washington, D.C., as the director of operational requirements. In essence, he became one of Arnold's close advisers. After his arrival, Doolittle was immediately sent into the field to evaluate the Martin B-26 Marauder, a medium-size bomber. Doolittle quickly quelled the complaints that the B-26 was too unforgiving for the average pilot. Before he was done with the B-26, Doolittle had the aircrew flying it on a single engine and had built their confidence to extremely high levels. He recommended that the newly renamed Army Air Forces continue to build the B-26, which it did.

While Doolittle was testing out the Marauder, FDR had secretly challenged the general staff to come up with a plan to attack the Japanese heartland.

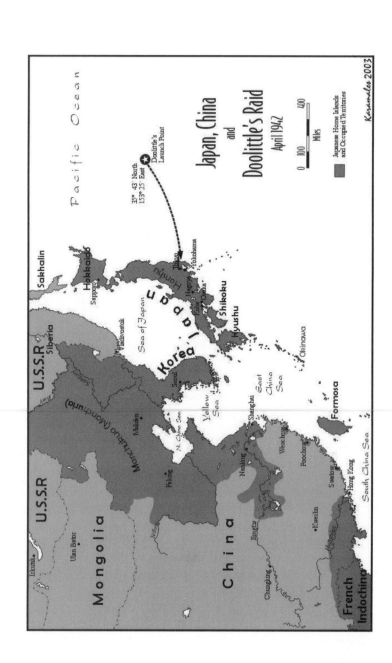

Chapter 5

The Raid

Aᴠᴛᴇʀ ᴊᴀᴘᴀɴᴇsᴇ carrier-based airpower dealt a stunning tactical blow to U.S. military forces in Hawaii, "instant hatred" enveloped America.[1] FDR became a wartime president. One of his most immediate concerns was to initiate a retaliatory strike against the Japanese.[2]

By mid-January 1942, the concept of a carrier-based strike had been accepted as the most plausible solution to FDR's earlier request. Capt. Francis S. Low, a submariner, had approached Adm. Ernest J. King, Chief of Naval Operations, and suggested that Army Air Forces bombers might successfully launch from a carrier and strike Japan from beyond the effective range of their land-based fighters. King sent him to Navy Capt. Donald B. "Wu" Duncan, his air operations officer, to evaluate the possibilities for such a plan. Arnold assigned Lieutenant Colonel Doolittle to work with Wu Duncan, as most of the preliminaries would take place in the War Department.

"The original plan," Doolittle stated in his official report to Hap Arnold, "was to take off and return to an aircraft carrier. Takeoff and landing tests conducted with three B-25Bs at

Norfolk, Virginia, indicated that takeoff from the carrier would be comparatively easy but landing back on again extremely difficult."[3] Once carrier landings had been ruled out, possible recovery fields on the Asian mainland were considered. Vladivostok was the best option, as it was only six hundred statute miles from Tokyo. Doolittle recalled that "the Russians were having real trouble on the Western Front, and the last thing in the world they wanted was conflict on their Eastern Front. So the Russians refused us permission to go to Vladivostok."[4] That development left only Chinese airfields for landing—some 1,200 statute miles from the target. Following the mission, the bombers were to remain in Chinese hands as part of the AQUILA detachment that was being organized as the core element of U.S. airpower in China.[5]

On 31 January, Arnold directed Brig. Gen. Carl A. "Tooey" Spaatz, his deputy for intelligence, to begin selecting the targets for the raid and assemble the target study folders. Navy Lt. Cmdr. Stephen Jurika, an intelligence officer on the *Hornet*, had assembled these folders some time before. In 1939, Jurika had served as the Navy's air attaché to the American embassy in Tokyo. "I spent most of my time," Jurika recalled, "locating and pinpointing industries, industrial areas, and all manner of bomb target information."[6] Jurika had been a spy in the most traditional sense of the word, and now his experiences were being put to military use.

Doolittle quickly established the necessary requirements for the aircraft that might accomplish this mission—2,400 statute miles cruising range while carrying a 2,000-pound bomb load. Of the candidates, the North American B-25B Mitchell bomber was selected. Both the Army and the Navy had independently decided upon the B-25 for the mission after a brief but intense period of research. To verify their choice, three B-25s were immediately flown to Norfolk; two of them were used for carrier-takeoff testing. The Navy's newest aircraft carrier, *Hornet*, was due to arrive there on 31 January.

Immediately, twenty-four B-25B aircraft from the Seventeenth Bombardment Group were selected for modification and preflight preparation. Eighteen of these were originally planned to accomplish the raid, but only sixteen would fit on the deck of the carrier with enough room for takeoff. Five crews each were selected from the Thirty-fourth, Seventy-fifth, and Ninety-fifth Bombardment Squadrons and the Eighty-ninth Reconnaissance Squadron for the mission. The Seventeenth BG left Pendleton, Oregon, for Columbia, South Carolina, in February and by the first week in March had redeployed to Eglin Field in the panhandle of Florida.[7]

Eighteen B-25s flew to Minnesota and then Indiana, where they were all fitted with additional fuel tanks. The range of an unmodified Mitchell was only 1,300 statute miles on a good day.[8] These aircraft were going on a mission planned for at least two thousand statute miles. The McQuay Company and the United States Rubber Company installed a variety of tanks under the supervision of the Materiel Division of the Army Air Forces, then under the command of Brigadier General George C. Kenney. A 265-gallon steel tank was installed to fit half of the bomb bay. It was found unsatisfactory and replaced with a 225-gallon version. This rubber tank, encased in steel, experienced leaking difficulties until the day before the mission was launched. The size of this tank required a modification to the bomb-carriage mechanism. Devices were added to allow four five-hundred-pound bombs to hang underneath the newly installed tank.

Above the bomb bay, in the crawlway, there existed room for more fuel, so a 160-gallon collapsible rubber fuel bladder was installed. This tank was to be emptied first and then deflated and stowed out of the way as soon as possible after the mission began. Doolittle also approved the installation of another sixty-gallon leakproof tank—a two-foot cube—where the lower gun turret would have been. The weight of the guns was too much for a mission of such duration. Ten five-gallon cans of gas were stowed in the radio operator's seat. Several radio components had been removed to conserve 230 pounds since the mission was going to be executed under strict radio silence. When all was added together, 1,141 gallons of gasoline could be loaded in each aircraft. The predicted range for this amount of fuel was 2,400 statute miles at an altitude of 5,000 feet. This left just enough room for two thousand pounds of bombs.[9]

The highly secret Norden bombsight was removed. It was not very accurate at low altitude and, if captured by the Japanese, could have revealed classified bombsight technology. In its place was installed a simple metal aiming sight—about a foot long and looking more like a child's toy than a deadly part of a weapon system—developed by Capt. C. "Ross" Greening. In testing, the "Mark Twain" sight was far more accurate than any other low-altitude design in service at that time. The nickname was a parody of earlier bombsights—the Mark II and the Mark XIV.[10]

Little ammunition was available for live firing the .50-caliber machine guns mounted in the upper turret. When testing did take place, the guns malfunctioned and constantly jammed. A Wright Field technician, W. C. Olson, replaced parts, machined pieces to fit more securely, and trained the gun-maintenance crews to clean and repair the weapons. By the time of the mission, most of the problems had been solved.

Cameras of two types were installed on the airplanes. For Doolittle's ship and each of the five flight leaders', "small electrically operated automatic cameras which took 60 pictures at one-half second intervals . . . were located at the extreme tip of the tail between the two wooden [replicas—they were actually broomsticks painted black] fifty caliber guns."[11] These still-frame cameras could be activated by the pilot and were automatically activated after bombs were dropped. The rest of the aircraft had motion-picture cameras mounted in the same location that operated in the same way.

The crews and airplanes met up with one another by 3 March at Eglin Field, where their training was to take place. Only the essentials were covered during those few weeks at Eglin. Cross-country techniques, night-flying procedures, and navigation took the most time. Low-altitude bombing, rapid escape, and target identification took another chunk of their time. The most intense training during March took place on a small auxiliary

Young Jimmy, circa 1905.
National Air and Space Museum

Rosa Doolittle and son, James Harold, Nome, Alaska.
National Air and Space Museum

Frank Henry Doolittle, Jimmy's carpenter father, circa 1905.
National Air and Space Museum

Lt. Jimmy Doolittle,
circa 1918.
*National Air and
Space Museum*

Daring and sometimes reckless in his early years, Doolittle kept an extensive photo record of his escapades. Here he is wing-walking on a biplane sometime around 1919.
National Air and Space Museum

The Rockwell Field low flying team in 1919 featured several young aviators including one Jimmy Doolittle, second from right.
Robert Arnold Collection

On September 4 and 5, 1921, Jimmy set the transcontinental record flying from Florida to California in less than twenty-four hours for the first time. As if to say, "One leg down, one to go," Jimmy hops out of his modified DH-4B in San Antonio—the only fueling stop on the way to California.
National Air and Space Museum

Billy Mitchell (center) stands on the deck of the *Alabama* after his Martin bombers attacked the ship during September 1921.
Robert Arnold Collection

A Martin Bomber explodes a phosphorus bomb over one of the 1921 test ships. *Robert Arnold Collection*

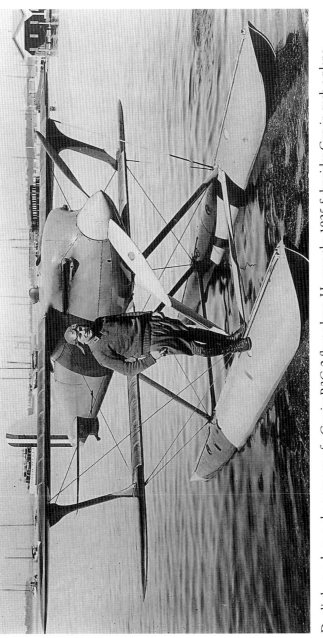

Doolittle stands atop the pontoon of a Curtiss R3C-2 float plane. He won the 1925 Schneider Cup in such a plane.
National Air and Space Museum

Doolittle wrecked this Navy Vought Corsair O2U-1 while returning to Mitchell Field after a cross-country instrument practice flight. This aircraft was not equipped for bad weather landings. Amazingly, he walked away uninjured. *National Air and Space Museum*

Jimmy in the cockpit of the Consolidated NY-2 used during his "blind" landing experiments. Doolittle pioneered instrument flying procedures, including the best locations for important instruments. *National Air and Space Museum*

Doolittle eyes the result of one of his many crashes. The landing gear on this Laird LC-DW 500 "Super Solution" would not extend. The damage was too severe for quick repairs leaving him without a plane for the 1931 Thompson race.
National Air and Space Museum

In the 1920s and early 1930s, Doolittle was a big name for a growing company—Shell.
National Portrait Gallery, Smithsonian Institution

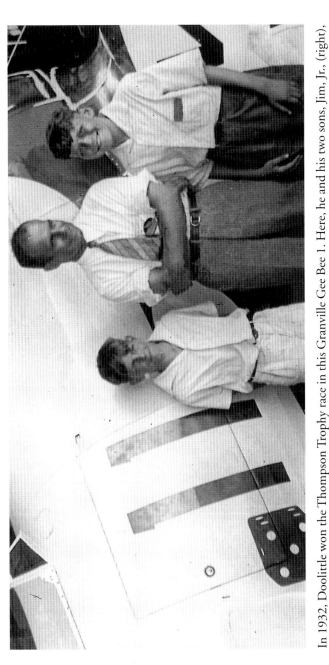

In 1932, Doolittle won the Thompson Trophy race in this Granville Gee Bee 1. Here, he and his two sons, Jim, Jr., (right), and John (left), pose for a few photos. Doolittle suffered a tremendous personal tragedy when Jim, Jr. took his own life in 1958. *National Air and Space Museum*

On April 18, 1942, Jimmy led a flight of sixteen B-25B Mitchell bombers in what would become one of the most famous and daring military operations in history, the Tokyo Raid. Note the full flap extension on Doolittle's airplane necessary to lift the normally land-based bomber off the deck of the aircraft carrier.
National Air and Space Museum

Jimmy's B-25 wreckage was scattered all over the rugged hillside "somewhere in China." Only one of the sixteen aircraft landed on its wheels and they were in Russia. The rest crash landed or bailed out.
Air Force Association

Maj. Gen. Doolittle took command of the Fifteenth Air Force on
November 1, 1943.
National Air and Space Museum

Lt. Gen. Doolittle confers with Gen. Hap Arnold, commanding general, U.S. Army Air Forces, 1944.
Robert Arnold Collection

runway, about five miles from the main landing field—aux field #9.[12] Navy Lt. Henry L. "Hank" Miller was selected to teach each crew the finer points of carrier takeoff procedures. Practice began by using a near-empty aircraft. Once success was achieved, the weight load was increased until, finally, launches using an overloaded 31,000-pound B-25 were accomplished by each crew. For the takeoff, the bomber was configured with flaps full down, three-fourths stabilizer trim set "tail-heavy," full power set against the brakes until the engines simultaneously reached their maximum revolutions—in layman's terms, to get airborne as quickly as humanly possible. The most unnerving part of the launch was the positioning of the control column. It was "pulled back gradually and the airplane left the ground with the tail skid about one foot from the runway. . . . The airplane took off almost in a stall."[13] The acceptable standard for a successful run was dependent upon aircraft weight and prevailing winds. At its heaviest, a B-25 using proper technique in a ten-knot headwind became airborne at about eight hundred feet. Miller computed that the wind component would be at least triple that at sea.[14]

Doolittle's instructors and flight leaders had the crews ready in a mere three weeks. "Ski" York, Doolittle's operations officer, had overseen the qualification process while Jimmy had been back and forth to Washington, D.C., in conference with Arnold. The flyers were not perfect, but it was all the time they had to prepare. Doolittle had personally qualified during the first week in March. That week was Jimmy's first flight in a B-25. While the B-25 crews trained in Florida, *Hornet* commanding officer, Capt. Marc A. Mitscher, had sailed south, then west through the Panama Canal, then up the West Coast to Alameda, California—Doolittle's boyhood home.

On 25 March, the modified B-25s headed for California. They had all arrived at the Sacramento Air Depot by the 27th for final inspections, last-minute installations of crew survival equipment and pristine propellers. By 1 April, the bombers had flown from Sacramento to Alameda Naval Air Station. The copilot for the number eight plane recalled that after landing from their one-hour shakedown flight, they taxied the B-25 right out to the dock where the aircraft carrier *Hornet* was waiting. From there, each plane was carefully lifted aboard the carrier and lashed to the deck.[15]

Doolittle returned to Washington, D.C., during these busy weeks, partly because of the secrecy involved in the project but also because he was still technically assigned as one of General Arnold's advisers. There were, however, a few occasions when Jimmy was forced to call Arnold directly. These occurred when outside agencies—the Sacramento Air Depot in particular—failed to act with the urgency required during modification and training to meet the compressed mission time line. It wasn't surprising, then, that after a quick call from Arnold, work proceeded at a pace that Doolittle would accept.

Over the years, there has been some discussion about whether Doolittle was actually selected to lead the Tokyo Raid when it was conceived. Jimmy's autobiography recalls a slapstick sequence of events that took place between him, Hap Arnold, and Millard "Miff" Harmon, Arnold's chief of staff. Doolittle recalls "selling" Arnold on the idea of leading the raid himself and then racing to Harmon's office to verify Arnold's approval before he could change his mind.[16] There may be some truth in this story, as Hap Arnold often played practical jokes on those closest to him.

If not Doolittle, who would lead? Jimmy had organized the Army Air Forces side of the raid from the beginning. He knew all the technical details. He was the only individual involved in planning who was aware of the true "commander's intent" behind the raid. Jimmy was not just the administrative leader; he was the chief of morale and was revered by all those who had volunteered. In Arnold's mind, once the final plan was revealed, there was never a doubt that Doolittle would lead the attack.

In his autobiography, Arnold recalled that the decision to use Lieutenant Colonel Doolittle was a "natural one." He stated that the fearless, technically brilliant officer, the same one he had grounded for stunting some twenty years earlier, "not only could be counted upon to do a task himself if it were humanly possible, but could impart this spirit to others." Even facing what Arnold called a "suicidal mission," Doolittle got things done.[17]

Additionally, Jimmy worked near Arnold in the War Department. The secrecy of this mission required close-hold communications, and close proximity made leaks less likely. Doolittle's ability to solve difficult problems, an ability that had developed since his early biplane experiences, was perfect for this mission. This combination of factors was the reason Jimmy was selected to lead the raid over other highly qualified pilots.

Part of the plan was to demonstrate a carrier takeoff before the mission was launched. For that purpose, a sixteenth B-25 was loaded onto the *Hornet.* Adm. William F. Halsey had turned down Doolittle's request for each pilot to practice one carrier takeoff before he set sail. The time required would have been unacceptable. Halsey did agree to allow one crew to take off from the carrier once it was out to sea and return to the West Coast, weather permitting. Later, confident from the takeoff trials on the East Coast, that aircraft was added to the mission and the at-sea test was not undertaken. In fact, all the AAF pilots were convinced that the takeoff could be safely accomplished.[18] Navy leadership, apparently, was not so sure. When asked by Commander in Chief, Pacific Fleet, Adm. Chester W. Nimitz if the raid could work, Halsey replied, "They'll need a lot of luck."[19] As it turned out, he was right.

As the planes were loaded, the crew members and their support personnel reported for duty on the ship. Lieutenant Miller had instructed them on the proper etiquette for "coming aboard," and they did so in a crisp and respectable fashion. The ship unmoored and anchored in the middle of San Francisco Bay the evening of 1 April 1942.[20] Doolittle, after giving the men a reminder about the total secrecy of the mission, released them to go ashore for dinner and a night on the town. Most ended up, after a few detours, at a classy, high-rise restaurant—the Top of the Mark. From there, they could see the *Hornet* and all their airplanes floating in the middle of the bay, and so could any enemy sympathizers who cared to look.

Jimmy had called Joe to San Francisco and had been spending as much time with her as he could. On the morning of 2 April, he kissed her good-bye, told her he would be "out of the country for a while," and returned to the *Hornet* to begin the operational phase of the mission. He wondered if he would see her again.[21] In the wee hours of the morning, the men had returned to the ship and prepared for departure. Right around noon, the *Hornet* passed beneath the Golden Gate Bridge and soon joined the rest of the Task Force ships that had set sail earlier.

Gen. George Marshall and Gen. Hap Arnold sent telegrams of encouragement and well wishes. Marshall even called Jimmy as the *Hornet* was sailing from the bay and made his message more personal. Later, Mitscher made the announcement to all aboard the *Hornet* that they were bound for Tokyo. A monumental cheer went up, and the anticipation of what awaited the Task Force began.[22]

Training awaited the bomber crews. For the next sixteen days, Doolittle gave lectures on mission procedures, Lieutenant Commander Jurika gave briefings on Asian culture, and Dr. (1st Lt.) Thomas R. White (AAF), the flight surgeon, gave informative talks on sanitation and first aid. Gunnery procedures were reviewed, and expert naval navigators gave refresher celestial-navigation training to B-25 navigators. Live-fire gunnery was practiced off the deck of the *Hornet* by shooting at target kites that were flown behind the ship. The mechanics spent much of their time with the planes. Propellers were rotated daily while checks for fluid leaks and other system malfunctions were also accomplished. The salt air and the pitching of the deck, coupled with lack of use during the journey, was not optimal treatment for the aircraft. "You don't just load them on and let them set there," said the youngest crew member of the attack force, aircraft mechanic Joseph Manske.[23]

There was some leisure time during the journey. The officers played craps on a large billiard table in the recreation room. Pilot Davey Jones, mission navigation and intelligence officer, found such a recreational addition laughable: "What in the world are you doing with a billiard table on a SHIP?"[24]

Several attack plans had been studied and restudied. Doolittle's original concept was for a daylight raid after a night launch from the carrier. Naval planners, however, considered the problems associated with night operations too risky, and that plan was scrapped. The second plan consisted of a dawn departure, a daylight raid, and then landing at dusk at Chinese airfields. This idea was shelved as fears over daylight detection mounted among the planners. The plan the Army and the Navy finally agreed upon included a near-dusk takeoff and a night raid on Tokyo. This option, it was thought, stood the best chance of achieving surprise under the "greater security of a night attack."[25] The plan depended upon a fast carrier run-in at night to get as close to the mainland as possible just prior to launch and then an immediate turn back toward Hawaii and a run for waters beyond the range of Japanese land-based aircraft.

On 13 April, Task Force 16.2 met up with Task Force 16.1, Halsey's force, near Hawaii, and proceeded toward the Japanese mainland with a total of sixteen ships that included his flagship, the aircraft carrier *Enterprise*.[26] As Task Force 16 approached the launch point, Doolittle was planning to take off two hours ahead of the rest of the force, "fire the most inflammable part of the city with incendiary bombs," and, in so doing, light the way to the target for the rest of the bombers.[27] Doolittle planned to lead these sixteen planes and eighty men from the front. Such a plan, however, would have exposed the fifteen-ship main force to a prepared defense and blacked-out target cities. In retrospect, this plan was as tactically flawed as the daylight attack. Fortunately for the B-25 crews, they were forced to launch early.

Doolittle had designated flight leaders during training. That function was intended as an administrative one. Since the plan was for a night attack, there was never any plan to approach Japan while flying in close—wingtip-to-wingtip—formation. Maintaining a perfect position next to another aircraft in flight, although not excessively difficult, requires continual diligence and attention by the pilots flying on the wing. Most critical for this mission were the continual small changes needed in throttle setting. It was commonly acknowledged that since the leader did not need to change his throttle settings and the wingman was constantly doing so, fuel consumption for the wingman was always greater than that of the leader. Fuel considerations for this mission being what they were, close-formation flying was never considered viable. But a loose-formation technique, trailing slightly behind and to the side of another by three to five miles, was practical. Throttle settings between the airplanes were quite evenly matched, and in-flight visibility, and daylight conditions, allowed maintenance of such visual contact. This technique was used at times during the raid by several of Doolittle's pilots but was not part of the original plan.[28]

The night-attack plan was disrupted when Japanese picket boats spotted Task Force 16 early on the morning of the 18th. While in San Francisco, Doolittle and Halsey had discussed the details of the mission, including the possibility of early detection by enemy forces. Several options for the B-25s were discussed, but the bottom-line agreement was that "if we were intercepted by Japanese surface craft, we would clear [*Hornet's*] decks in order that the task force could protect themselves . . . one way or another." Of the possibilities discussed, the force had reached the outer limits of the attack range and so there were no other acceptable options; to protect Task Force 16, the mission was launched immediately.[29]

According to Doolittle's after-action report to General Arnold, the Raiders began taking off from 35' 43" north longitude and 153' 25" east latitude. If these coordinates are accurate, they were almost exactly 750 nautical miles from Tokyo when they launched. The distance from Tokyo to the planned landing fields in China was 1,230 nautical miles, making the total flight 1,980 nautical miles. Air planning was accomplished in statute miles, however, and the total distance of 2,275 statute miles was beyond the requirements demanded by combat maneuvering, low-altitude flying, and required fuel reserves. The reality was that they did not have enough gas, without some kind of help, to make it to their planned landing bases after flying the combat mission. Halsey's insistence and Doolittle's agreement to launch the attack protected Halsey's fleet from a potentially debilitating aerial attack but condemned the Raiders to an uncertain fate.

Vice Adm. Matoi Ugaki, commander of the combined Japanese forces responsible for that sector, had issued orders to intercept and engage Task Force 16. By the time the Japanese could launch the attack, however, Halsey had deposited Doolittle's planes, turned his ships, and was dashing well out of the range of Japanese attack aircraft.[30] Task Force 16 suffered no casualties from enemy activity even though they had operated in the enemy's backyard. Protection of the Navy's limited carrier assets was essential since the Navy had not yet recovered from the Japanese attack at Pearl Harbor.

While all the Army crews were reporting to their planes, protective tarpons were removed and fuel cans were filled and stowed aboard. The day before the anticipated launch, during ceremonies on board the *Hornet*, Doolittle had affixed military medals given to sailors by the Japanese during peacetime to the five-hundred-pound bombs destined for Japanese targets. These bombs had already been loaded aboard pilot Ted Lawson's number seven bomber. Ominous final instructions were given: "avoid non-military targets, particularly the Temple of Heaven, and even though we were put off so far at sea that it would be impossible to reach the China coast, not to go to Siberia but to proceed as far west as possible, land on the water, launch the rubber boat and sail in." The crews were also admonished not to destroy the tall radio towers in the Tokyo area.[31] Planners wanted to be sure that news of the attack could be widely disseminated to the Japanese people across the radio waves.

Essentially, owing to the added distance at the takeoff point, there was no certain plan for how or where to land these aircraft when Doolittle took off at 8:20 A.M. ship's time. When Jimmy's B-25 rose from the *Hornet*'s undulating deck, he already knew the mission was in jeopardy and might end under a billowing parachute or trying to escape from a sinking plane at sea.[32] Halsey and Doolittle shared in the responsibility for the launch decision, and they acted with the clear intention of completing the mission as FDR had demanded. It remained unspoken but understood that the bombardment of Tokyo had become more important than the eighty lives or the sixteen airplanes involved.

The *Hornet* steered into the wind while the deck pitched in heavy seas. Engines roared to life, and Doolittle taxied his plane forward a few feet onto three cork pads that had been laid to provide enough friction for the tires to hold the B-25 stationary as the engines were pushed to full throttle. Takeoff procedures worked as advertised, and once safely airborne, each plane accelerated and then made a climbing, 360-degree clockwise turn so as to fly directly over the deck of the *Hornet*. This vital procedure was how the B-25 navigators aligned their compasses to ensure the best possible heading information for the longer-than-planned trip to Japan. "This was considered necessary and desirable," Doolittle reported, "due to the possibility of change in compass calibration, particularly on those ships that were located close to the island."[33] Jimmy understood the importance of this instrument from his blind-flying experiments in 1929.

One by one, each aircraft accomplished the launch procedure. Only two glitches occurred. The number seven plane piloted by Ted Lawson took off without its flaps properly positioned. Miraculously, the plane made it airborne after a nerve-racking, sinking departure from the end of the deck. As the last aircraft was preparing to take off, an unfortunate gust of prop wash hit a deckhand and he lost his footing on the slippery surface. Lt. William G. "Bill" Farrow's whirling portside propeller nearly sliced off his left arm. It was a sickening sound, like paper hitting a fan, but there was no time for sorrow. The last crew never got to align their compass due to a minor aircraft-control problem while flying over the carrier deck.[34]

Each of the sixteen B-25s was responsible for specific targets. The actual attack plan was much more tactically complicated than history reflects. From Doolittle's official report to Gen. Hap Arnold:

> All pilots were given selected objectives, consisting of steel works, oil refineries, oil tank farms, ammunition dumps, dock yards, munitions plants, airplane factories, etc. They were also given secondary targets in case it was impossible to reach the primary target. . . . In addition to each plane having selected targets assigned to it, each flight was assigned a specific course and coverage. The first flight of 3 airplanes, led by Lt. Travis Hoover, covered the Northern part of Tokyo. The second flight, led by Captain [David M. "Davey"] Jones, covered the central part of Tokyo. The third flight, led by Captain York, covered the southern part of Tokyo and the north central part of the Tokyo Bay area. The fourth flight, led by Capt. Greening, covered the southern part of Kenegawa, the city of Yokahama and the Yokosuka Navy Yard. The flight was spread over a 50-mile front in order to provide the greatest possible coverage, to create the impression that there were a larger number of airplanes than were actually used, and to dilute enemy ground and air fire. It also prohibited the possibility of more than one plane passing any given spot on the ground and assured the element of surprise. . . . The fifth flight [led by Major John A. Hilger] went around to the South of Tokyo and proceeded to the vicinity of Nogoya [*sic*] where it broke up, one plane bombing Nagoya, one Osaka and one Kobe.[35]

Doolittle's mission objective was to ignite fires for the rest to follow, but that element of the plan was unnecessary. The sun was shining brightly about half-past noon when Jimmy became the first pilot to bomb the Japanese homeland in fulfillment of FDR's orders.

Getting to the targets was not as easy as Doolittle's report made it sound. After planes had traveled more than seven hundred statute miles, minuscule errors in heading control were amplified, putting planes many miles off course. Several of the B-25 crews were totally lost when they finally made landfall right around noon. Doolittle flew well north of his planned route, but quick work by his navigator, Henry Potter, steered him back on course—much to the relief of those following him in trail. After a quick climb to obtain a visual fix, the temporarily misoriented bombers caught a glimpse of Tokyo Bay and were oriented once again. Manske wondered why they were flying over Japanese soil for so long a time. "It turned out my pilot didn't know where he was at."[36] This demonstrated how well the bomber crews were trained to handle what Clausewitz referred to as friction in war.[37]

"Friction" may be an understatement. The plan had been splintered by the Japanese detection of the fleet. This resulted in a daylight launch and jeopardized the possibility of a safe landing. Compass drift and winds had pushed most of the aircraft well off their planned course. Unknown to the Raiders, the one aircraft that carried the homing radio beacons for the landing fields in China had crashed and taken with it any chance of finding the strips at night or in bad weather. Lastly, but fortunately, the original targets, planned for night recognition and attack, were large industrial zones, and hitting at least some part of the complex would be much easier during broad daylight.

The question of American bombing doctrine must here be raised. The final plans for this raid centered on a night attack. The American bombardment doctrine with which the AAF entered the air war was one of precision, high-altitude, daylight bombing. None of these precepts were followed in the planning or the subsequent execution of the Tokyo Raid. Why?

This raid was not intended to do maximum damage; rather, it was intended to make a spectacle.[38] The attack was designed so that the Japanese people would clearly know that a foreign enemy had bombed Tokyo. The fires Doolittle had planned to set were not only to serve as beacons to the other fifteen B-25s but also to dramatically, and undeniably, announce that the capital city had been bombed. The plan to spread the attack force over a fifty-mile front, at night, would have created the effect of many, perhaps hundreds of aircraft, attacking the island. Further, the order forbidding the bombardment of the radio towers near Tokyo revealed that immediate dissemination of the news by Japanese radio was expected. This was exactly what FDR had in mind when he ordered the attack.

It was not doctrine but flexible, creative thinking that generated such an audacious plan. In reality, the Doolittle Raid violated almost every accepted doctrinal idea for bombardment openly held by the AAF. Ironically, another airman charged by Arnold to bomb Japan resorted to the same strategy, low-altitude firebombing, during the spring of 1945—that was Curtis E. LeMay. Doolittle understood, as did many who had never attended the Air Corps Tactical School—including the naval officers who had conceived the plan in the first place—that bombing doctrine was a guide, not a law. The mission objective, in this case a psychological one, dictated the method. Doolittle, later as commander of Eighth Air Force in Europe, remembered that lesson.

The reality was, however, that the raid occurred in daylight. Postmission reports revealed that the number two B-25, able to see Doolittle's plane, actually flew a three-mile trail-type formation behind him all the way to the target area—even when Jimmy accomplished an evasive left turn to avoid a Japanese ship during the flight to the mainland. The second flight of three (numbers five, six, and seven) flew a loose formation all the way until they reached the mainland and, after locating their target area, split up for the attack. Two of them regained sight after the attack and followed each other until they made the westerly turn toward China. Numbers fourteen and fifteen flew in formation all the way to the target area. They expected the number sixteen airplane to tag along as well, but they lost sight of one another during one of many rainstorms between the carrier and the coast. By practicing this basic form of mutual combat support, it is likely that those following Doolittle, admittedly lost when they reached Japan, were steered to the target area by Doolittle's excellent navigator.[39]

Doolittle reported that "in almost every case primary targets were bombed. The damage done far exceeded our most optimistic expectations. The high degree of damage resulted from the highly inflammable nature of Japanese construction, the low altitude from which the bombing was carried out . . . the perfectly clear weather over Tokyo, and the careful and continuous study of charts and target areas."[40] In addition, different planes carried different combinations of bombs depending on their targets. Doolittle carried four five-hundred-pound incendiary cluster bombs since Jurika had selected a particularly inflammable area for him to attack. Others, whose targets were industrial in nature, carried three demolition bombs and one incendiary cluster in hopes that after the damage was done a tremendous fire might ignite. The mission plan demonstrated many conventional elements of sound military strategic and tactical thought: surprise, economy of force, audacity, and deception. The entire premise, however, clearly violated accepted AAF doctrine—that of strategic, daylight, precision bombardment.

The execution of the raid under rapidly changing circumstances may be more remarkable an achievement than even legend holds. Eighty airmen and their planes, not sure of the endgame for the mission, improvising formations and targeting, carefully calculating mileage from gas supplies well below the levels expected, followed Jimmy Doolittle into total uncertainty. Of Doolittle's many accomplishments, planning this mission and executing it under the pressures of war demonstrated a true mastery of calculation versus risk. It had taken more than twenty years for Jimmy to reach such a pinnacle of aerial achievement and leadership.

Mission reports received from Doolittle's crews varied in their accounts of encounters with enemy ground fire and fighter defenses. A few saw enemy fighters that did not attack, a few were attacked but ineffectively, and in at least one case the bullets fired by the Japanese plane simply bounced off the skin of the B-25. Anti-aircraft fire was inaccurate. Doolittle credited the high-speed, low-level approach and attack with destroying the gunners' aim. The Japanese had lofted barrage balloons in the vicinity of Tokyo. These balloons carried chains into the air and could have ripped an airplane apart had one flown into the deadly trap.

The daylight helped the pilots avoid such defenses easily. Flak bursting near these barrage balloons actually destroyed several of them in fiery explosions that added to the spectacle.[41]

Doolittle's raid succeeded in accomplishing its mission. Only one aircraft, number four, released its bombs harmlessly into Tokyo Bay and only after it was attacked twice by Japanese fighters. Of the others, at least four missed their primary targets for a variety of reasons. They bombed either their secondary target or a target of opportunity that appeared to be industrial or military in nature. The rest claimed direct hits—which was not surprising since the targets were very large complexes. Weapons were released anywhere between 600 and 2,500 feet above the ground. No official bomb damage assessment was accomplished by American forces, but news photographs later revealed graphic damage after the raid. The fact that four of the sixteen planes missed their primary target can be attributed to navigation errors and evasive maneuvering during the journey. These were largely induced by compass precession (small shifts in the magnetic heading) after a long flight over the ocean and unknowable winds where no course updates could be made. Additionally, bomber pilots were forced to react to rapidly changing combat situations, like attacks by enemy fighters, finding their targets from new directions, and dodging anti-aircraft fire.

All sixteen planes had descended to extremely low altitude to egress the target area at high speed. All sixteen crews began the task of calculating how much fuel they had remaining and how far they could fly with that reserve. Initial calculations were not encouraging. Davey Jones's navigator, Lt. Eugene F. McGurl, sardonically quipped, "Hey, I don't think we're gonna have to swim more than one-hundred miles."[42]

Doolittle's luck continued that evening. A stiff tailwind had developed between Japan and China and, much to the surprise of the navigators, several of the planes appeared to be getting pretty good gas mileage and making pretty good time. Only one bomber had insufficient fuel to make it to the Chinese mainland, and it diverted to Russia rather than risk having to ditch in the middle of the North China Sea. Ski York's plane was the only aircraft to land on its wheels, and the five crewmen were interned in Russia until they managed to escape into Iran in May 1943.[43]

In retrospect, the course taken by this crew may have been the best solution for all the Raiders. Had Doolittle landed his force near Vladivostok, it is likely that all the crew would have survived and the Russians would have impounded the planes in an effort to emphasize their neutrality to the Japanese. The choice not to land in Russia, even without permission, was based upon political fears, not military practicality.

Once Jimmy's plane made landfall over China, his luck ran out. Since the Japanese had occupied much of coastal China, there were limited opportunities for landing at friendly airfields. Fearing air raids by the Japanese, and not knowing of the timing of the raid on the Japanese capital, when the B-25 engines were heard, people extinguished all lights on the ground. Doolittle reported that "this, together with the very unfavorable flight weather over the China Coast, made safe landing at destinations impossible. As a result all planes either landed in the water near the coast or the crews bailed out with their parachutes."[44]

Perhaps the greatest miscalculation of the mission was failing to notify indigenous U.S. Army forces of the details of the attack. Col. Claire L. Chennault, commander of the Flying Tigers in the service of the Chinese, had advanced the East China Air Warning network to a workable system. Had Chennault known more than the vagaries of the mission, postmission options might have been dramatically different from history records. It was a clear case of the desire for secrecy being detrimental to the successful recovery of the B-25s after the mission.[45]

Jimmy briefed his crew to prepare to bail out of their B-25. Doolittle's copilot, Richard E. Cole, recalled their discussion concerning the possibilities of escaping the plane. If crippled over the Japanese mainland, Doolittle did not intend to be captured. "I'm going to bail my crew out," he said, "and then dive it, full throttle, into any target I can find where the crash will do the most damage."[46] Later, as they approached the Chinese coast, the crew prepared to ditch, but Jimmy was looking for a friendly ship. If one could be found, he had considered landing near it so that his crew could be rescued. Doolittle, thinking out loud, suggested that even if the ship were not friendly, it would be better to ditch nearby and try to take the ship by force. These desperate proposals were unnecessary when the wind carried them well into China, where they performed a successful bailout. It was Jimmy's third parachute jump from an aircraft.[47]

After his crew was gathered together by a lone Chinese soldier, Doolittle spent the next few weeks negotiating with local authorities to retrieve the crewmen who had been captured by the Japanese. The attempt was unsuccessful. By chance, Doolittle's crew was introduced to an American missionary, John M. Birch.[48] Birch had been sent to the place where Jimmy and his boys were hiding out. It was Birch who helped the downed crewmen get started on their journey to safety.[49] Eventually, Jimmy linked up with Claire Chennault's forces and was notified of his immediate promotion from lieutenant colonel to brigadier general. On 30 April, Generalissimo Chiang Kai-shek and Madame Chiang decorated Doolittle's airmen and honored Jimmy and his deputy, Jack Hilger, with the Yon-Hwei, China's highest military award. An emphatic letter from the generalissimo to the State Department accompanied this act of goodwill, describing the atrocities of the Japanese offensive in the coastal areas of China.[50]

By early May, the Raiders were being reassigned to other jobs. Some remained in China, others came back to the United States, and others were destined for flying, fighting, and dying in Europe. Exhausted, Jimmy Doolittle returned to Washington, D.C.

The attack on Tokyo blurred the rules that defined mission success and failure. General Arnold cringed at the loss of all sixteen B-25s during the mission and, in that regard, considered the attack a failure. The loss of men and equipment, however, was necessarily weighed against political and strategic impact before the mission was launched. In the weeks following the raid, American morale appeared to soar. Militarily and on the home front, the war against Japan had taken a decidedly vengeful character—a character that sought retribution against a dastardly, even subhuman enemy.[51]

For the Chinese, the Tokyo Raid was cataclysmic. The Japanese vented their anger upon those who provided aid to the Raiders during their escape. Some 250,000 Chinese soldiers and peasants were massacred by invading Japanese air and ground forces during the next four months as the Japanese pushed their invasion deeper into China.

Doolittle's raid is a paradox in many respects. The North American B-25 bomber nicknamed Mitchell—for Billy Mitchell, the man who had predicted the Japanese attack on Hawaii during his court martial in 1925—was the chosen AAF weapon for the raid. AAF medium bombers were launched from a Navy carrier, an activity for which they were never designed. The night firebombing attack, a clear AAF doctrinal violation, was determined the best option for success but was scrapped to protect Task Force 16 from a possible enemy encounter. The Raid targeted inflammable areas around Tokyo in an attempt to send a message rather than cause extensive destruction of one particular industrial system—another bombing doctrine violation. The specific message from the Raiders to the people of Tokyo was cleanly and clearly painted on one of the bombs and was loaded with its words visibly facing the earth when the bomb bay was opened. It read, "I don't want to set the world on fire—just Tokyo."[52] The sentiment was eventually realized when LeMay's B-29s dropped incendiary bombs and destroyed much of the city in 1945.

Landing in China, even in the face of anticipated Japanese reprisal, won out over landing in Russia unwelcome and unannounced, despite the fact that Stalin's Russia was one of the Allies. Further, the only other real target that Jimmy had ever bombed before was the USS *Alabama* during the Mitchell bombing trials. He, along with all his Raiders, had no combat experience at all.

Despite these inconsistencies, the Tokyo Raid delivered the retaliatory blow that Americans had been anticipating since 7 December 1941. The raid also indirectly provided additional fuel, news of the Japanese slaughter of innocent Chinese, that fed the intense anti-Japanese fire then raging across America. This sentiment deepened in late October 1942, when news arrived of the execution of three of the Raiders who had been captured by the Japanese Army. Ironically, there was little uproar over Russia's refusal to allow the Raiders to land in Vladivostok.

The Doolittle Raid was Jimmy's first and, at that time, only combat mission. For his planning, execution, and leadership during the raid, he received the nation's highest military award. Arnold secretly sent for Joe, who was in California, and upon her arrival in Washington, she was swiftly escorted by car to the White House, where she met up with Arnold, Marshall, and Jimmy. Just after the cherry blossoms had fallen from the trees on 19 May 1942, President Franklin Delano Roosevelt, the man who had ordered the mission, personally decorated the newly promoted brigadier general, James H. Doolittle, with the Medal of Honor in a private White House ceremony. During a time when America was desperately seeking a hero, FDR gave the country Doolittle.[53]

Despite the many ironies, one uniquely American ideal had been demonstrated by the execution of the Tokyo Raid—civil control of the military. The president had specifically directed that such an attack be carried out against Japan. America's military had embraced and then followed those orders as directed. There is no irony in the fact that the air war's first battle over Japan was as politically directed as the ultimate air attack ordered by President Harry Truman—incineration of two Japanese cities with atomic weapons in August 1945.

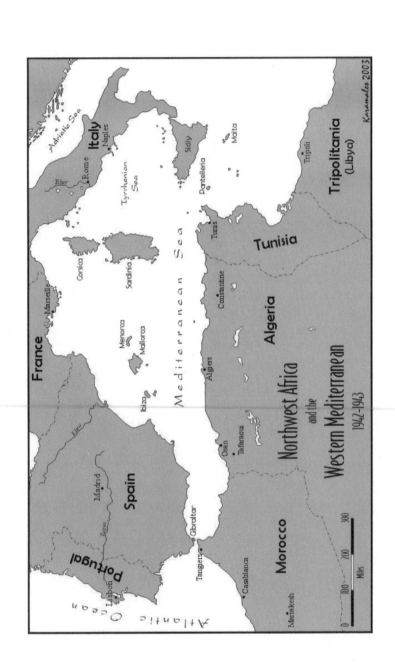

Northwest Africa

and the

Western Mediterranean

1942-1943

Kraemer 2003

Chapter 6

World War II: The Young General

AFTER HE WAS presented with the Medal of Honor, Doolittle began to fulfill his mission as a presidentially anointed national hero. Jimmy never considered himself one. If anything, the award of the medal humbled and motivated him to a higher level of energy and greater desire to perform well for those he served. He was immediately sent on a "morale building" tour of aircraft and aircraft-support factories. General Arnold gave him a B-25 as transportation—a symbol of the raid. Most important of his postraid tasks, to Jimmy anyway, was sending personal letters to every Raider's family. Each was different. Some were more difficult to write than others were. For some families, the fate of their loved ones was not yet known. For some, the news confirmed fears that loved ones had perished.

A good bit of his time was also spent answering congratulatory mail. Admiral Halsey's letter, sent to Washington from the Pacific a week after the raid, reflected the sentiment of most of the high command. In part it read:

> I am highly honored to have had you, and the very gallant and brave lads with you, serve under my command for a short period of time.

It is something I shall always remember. I do not know of any more gallant deed in history than that performed by your squadron, and that it was successful is entirely due to the splendid leadership on your part. It was a pleasure to meet you in San Francisco, and my immediate reaction was that I had met a real man. Events proved me right. You have struck the hardest blow of the war directly at the enemy's heart. You have made history.[1]

Halsey's euphoric tone may have been a premature outpouring of emotion. As a direct consequence of the Tokyo Raid, the Japanese decided to broaden their area of control in the Pacific. In June, the Japanese fleet under the command of Adm. Isoroku Yamamoto pushed its forces out as far as Midway. Pressed by the Japanese army, whose failure to defeat the B-25 attack had resulted in its humiliation, Yamamoto's existing plan to threaten Hawaii, already suspected by American naval intelligence experts, was hastily put into action. The plan had received tentative approval from Japan's Naval General Staff on 5 April, but the staff delayed action, fearing attacks from the Aleutians. After Doolittle's raid, there were no more arguments against Yamamoto's proposal.[2]

The first necessary move in extending the Japanese sphere of influence was to capture Midway Island. The blow inflicted upon the Japanese fleet and its air arm during the ensuing battle signaled an important turn of the tide in the Pacific Theater. While attacking the defenses around Midway during 4–6 June, the Japanese lost four aircraft carriers, one heavy cruiser, more than three hundred aircraft (more than two to one over American losses), and more than 2,100 men.[3] Doolittle's raid acted as a catalyst triggering these naval confrontations before the Japanese had fully prepared for them.

Jimmy Doolittle was already far away from ongoing operations in the Pacific. As with his flying career, his early years as a general started off rough. His first chance at command would have been back in the Pacific Theater. He and Maj. Gen. George C. Kenney had been nominated as candidates to fill the void as General MacArthur's air commander. Initially, Marshall had suggested Lt. Gen. Frank Andrews, then in command of the air forces protecting the Panama Canal. MacArthur, knowing of Andrews's reputation as a skilled air boss, accepted the offer. For a number of reasons, largely ones of potential personality conflict, Andrews suddenly became "unavailable" for the move that was considered a job demotion by most. Instead, MacArthur chose Kenney, a career air officer. Doolittle had no experience commanding large forces of planes and airmen. Largely because of that, MacArthur recognized that "it would be difficult to convince the Australians of Doolittle's acceptability."[4] The theatrical MacArthur and the abrasive Kenney somehow made an excellent team.

Brigadier General Doolittle was briefly assigned to command the Fourth Bombardment Wing (medium), part of the Eighth Air Force, then under the command of Maj. Gen. Carl A. "Tooey" Spaatz. Jimmy never commanded the unit because other war plans soon forced a change in the command structure for operations against Axis forces in Europe.

When plans for Operation Torch, the invasion of North Africa, were finalized, the air commander's slot needed filling. Both General Arnold and General Marshall recommended Doolittle. On 6 August, Jimmy and Maj. Gen. George S. Patton Jr., selected as the ground commander for Torch, went to London to discuss the military operation with Eisenhower. The meeting did not go well for Doolittle.

First, "Georgie" Patton described how his army would "murder those lousy Hun bastards by the bushel."[5] Lt. Gen. Eisenhower listened carefully to the briefing, then turned to Doolittle and told him what the objective for the Twelfth Air Force would be—to acquire airfields in North Africa and begin operations immediately. Making his first mistake at high command, Jimmy correctly but arrogantly pointed out that without logistical support, airfields would be useless. Eisenhower was a logistics master who needed no instruction in that area. Additionally, Jimmy held a reserve commission, while Eisenhower was a West Pointer, class of 1915. It was no surprise, then, that after their meeting Eisenhower wired Arnold to request another West Pointer, "Tooey" Spaatz, for the job, not an underling with minimal experience.[6]

Eisenhower, the overall invasion commander, wanted a general officer with experience in creating an air command. Arnold was forced to ask for Marshall's help in saving Jimmy's opportunity. After several discussions, Marshall finally wrote to Eisenhower on 12 September concerning Doolittle: "[Doolittle's] combination of industry, intensity, technical knowledge and level headed bearing has greatly impressed me as probably the outstanding leader type in our Air Corps."[7] Remarkably, Eisenhower was persuaded to change his mind. In his wartime memoir, Eisenhower commented that "it took [Doolittle] some time to reconcile himself to shouldering his responsibilities as the senior United States air commander [in North Africa] to the exclusion of opportunity for going out to fly a fighter plane against the enemy. But he had the priceless quality of learning from experience."[8] The decision to accept Doolittle demonstrated Eisenhower's trust in Marshall's judgment. Doolittle, with tremendous support from Arnold and Marshall, both of whom were present when FDR had pinned the Medal of Honor on his chest, took command of the Twelfth Air Force on 23 September 1942. Jimmy, much to his credit, recognized his shortcomings and inexperience as a commanding general. It took several months and help from an excellent staff to correct them.

Meanwhile, Jimmy set to the administrative tasks of organizing a new command. Initially, his forces consisted of two heavy-bombardment groups, two P-38 fighter groups, two Spitfire groups, one troop-carrier group, one light-bombardment group, and three medium-bombardment groups. These forces were consolidated from several sources, largely from the Eighth Air Force and units in the United States. During August and September this paper command was code-named Junior—as in Eighth Air Force Junior. Doolittle, for the most part, remained in London, but half of his command was in the States. Operational training was well under way in England, but the lack of a definitive command structure impaired Doolittle's ability to carry out his mission. Additionally, medium bomber assets and training for the crews were simply unavailable.[9] He prevailed upon George Patton to talk to Eisenhower about continued diversion of combat assets to other theaters. Patton did.[10]

Stateside, while hurried planning for Torch was well under way, Doolittle paid a personal visit to Arnold, who was already making the case that American airpower was being spread far too thin to support an invasion into North Africa. These were critical years for the Army Air Forces. Every theater air commander was asking for airplanes, and few were getting them. Many American-produced aircraft were sent to the British and other Allies as part of the lend-lease program. Arnold was responsible for directing assets to the places needed most at the right times. As a result of the combined pleas from Patton, Arnold, and Marshall, many needed planes eventually made their way from America and England to North Africa.

Doolittle's chief of staff was Col. Hoyt S. Vandenberg, a dashing chain-smoker destined for four-star rank. His deputy for operations (A-3) was Col. Lauris Norstad, a gifted planner and skilled staff officer. By surrounding himself with exceptional officers, Doolittle self-admittedly protected himself from making cataclysmic errors in judgment as he learned the business of generalship. He reflected this in his reports to Arnold:

> I have the best staff, the best commands and the smoothest-running organization in the Air Force. We are short as everyone else is, on experienced secondary personnel, but our key people are really tops. . . . Conditions in air warfare are changing so rapidly that our very inexperience is often an asset—we have little to forget.
>
> We have a job—a hard job—to do. We are looking forward with pleasant anticipation to the altogether successful accomplishment of it.[11]

Although internal operations seemed to be working well for Doolittle's command, the days from September until 8 November (D day for Operation Torch) were initially marked by inadequate communications between Allied air forces, poor operational planning and coordination for the invasion, and a lack of appropriate air assets. Doolittle reported to Eisenhower early in October that his forces were largely untrained or only partially trained for the upcoming mission. To minimize the impact of this shortfall, he proposed to use Eighth Air Force transfers as his front-line attack force while the new fliers received enough in-theater training to engage effectively in aerial combat. There was no doubt that some on-the-job training would also take place.[12] The morning after the ground forces had landed, Doolittle hopped into a B-17 and, escorted by Spitfires, flew to Tafaraoui and established his operational headquarters. Losses were light; more aircraft and crew were lost due to accidents and poor weather than to combat.

Although the Torch invasion landings had succeeded, the offensive stagnated and the ground campaign remained ineffectual until the following spring. When Jimmy reported back to Hap Arnold on 19 November, he gave much of the credit for these successes to those under his command. "An operation of this kind," Doolittle reported, "promptly separates the sheep from the goats and I am happy to report that all of our people showed up well and most of them were superior."[13] He also recommended those worthy for promotion and commended those who had performed exceptionally well during these months. Jimmy's "people skills" were improving. He had many lessons yet to learn, however, about high-level command.

It was also during this period that Doolittle received some personal instruction in generalship from Eisenhower. On one occasion, Jimmy had taken a British Spitfire IX for a test ride. While Doolittle was in the air, Eisenhower had attempted to contact him at his headquarters concerning a matter of some importance. Upon receiving the late summons, Jimmy immediately refueled and hopped to Eisenhower's headquarters at Gibraltar. After explaining to the perturbed Eisenhower that familiarity with his aircraft was crucial to "supervising people who flew airplanes," Jimmy was subjected to a military attitude adjustment. Eisenhower made clear Doolittle's function as an air commander. "I want my airmen available when I want them," Eisenhower said. "You can either be in command of my 12th Air Force, or you can be a second lieutenant and shoot down Germans, whichever you want to do." After that meeting Doolittle understood Eisenhower perfectly.[14] Eisenhower perceived Doolittle as a stronger field commander than an organizer. Events like this one demonstrated Jimmy's operational leadership above his personal involvement with administration, a task he left to his subordinate commanders.

Eisenhower could not have been too upset with Doolittle. Jimmy was promoted and pinned on his second star the same day his headquarters began its move from Tafaraoui—where the mud was "deep and gooey"—to Algiers on 30 November 1942.[15]

In January 1943, the Allies held a pivotal conference at Casablanca. It was during this meeting that the British argued for night area bombardment doctrine and the Americans defended daylight, precision, high-altitude bombing. The result was a scheme of round-the-clock bombing that defined and directed the air war until the Nazis surrendered. Part of the conference results also consolidated command structures in Europe and in North Africa. The organizational issues that affected operations in North Africa were ongoing even since before Doolittle took command of the newly established Twelfth Air Force in September 1942. These changes, largely the result of advances during the campaign and the consolidation of command of air and ground forces, directly impacted Doolittle's air command.

After several administrative reorganizations marrying the Middle East and the Northwest African theaters of war, Doolittle finally emerged as the commander for the Northwest African Strategic Air Forces (NASAF), a position he perceived as a demotion. In a letter to Joe, he explained, "I feel no resentment over the change. . . . I had the administrative, technical, and even the tactical side in hand. The latter achieved through competent staff and command personnel. On advertising and politics I was weak. . . . Politics! I have always sneered at the word 'politics.'"[16] Comprising several—sometimes four, then six—bomber groups, his new command was responsible for interdicting Axis supplies during the battle for Tunisia. In this, he was remarkably successful.

Doolittle's new force, a combined command, was composed of the XII Bomber Command and two RAF Wellington squadrons that were attached to their own supporting fighter forces. These aircraft were based on several airdromes around the city of Constantine, Doolittle's headquarters. "Tooey" Spaatz, the overall commander for the air forces in Northwest Africa (also given command of the Western Desert Air Forces in late February), established his operational headquarters near Doolittle's to keep in close touch during the campaign. Doolittle's command was only one part of a multifunction conglomeration of forces under Spaatz's command. In addition to the Strategic Command, there was the Tactical Command, the Coastal Air Force, the Training Command, and a Photographic Reconnaissance Wing, commanded by Col. Elliot Roosevelt.[17]

In broad terms, Doolittle's forces were to perform "tactical" missions—that is, missions in direct support of the ground forces. The interdiction of supplies also fell under this rubric. The official history of the AAF in World War II described the operations in North Africa during these winter months as merely "seasoning for all participating arms, British as well as American."[18] Some of the more important skills learned during these months were international cooperation and communications. Throughout the region since Casablanca, British and American officers were "interleaved," thus forcing command and culture to the altar under a watchful, shotgun-armed Spaatz.

From February until October 1943, Doolittle's forces skillfully interdicted enemy supplies throughout Italy. On at least six occasions, Doolittle flew with his men on these missions, but only the toughest ones. Doolittle was not a "milk run" commander. He led his airmen on tough missions from the front—by example. On most occasions he flew the temperamental B-26 medium bomber. He also flew missions in the B-17, B-25, P-38, and Spitfire as schedules allowed. On one occasion, his B-26 was narrowly missed by deadly flak just prior to the "bombs away" point. Two of his aircraft were shot down that day, and one was crippled by anti-aircraft fire.[19]

From February until May, when the city fell, Doolittle's forces routinely bombed Tunis. When Axis forces in North Africa surrendered on 13 May 1943, attacks turned to the boot of Italy and Germany. During July, the NASAF bombed communication and transportation targets in and around Rome, helping destroy Mussolini's grip on Italy. Doolittle's aircraft bombed Regensburg in what was the first strategic mission flown from the Mediterranean against the German homeland. His command was directly involved in the recovery and turnaround of Col. Curtis LeMay's bombers after the dismal raid against that target, taking weeks to repair the damaged planes.

All this time, Jimmy was learning the business of command—command on a scale that none had known before the massive military expansion that resulted from war. General Arnold had written, "The period that has taken the most out of me was the last three years [1942–44] when I was trying to perfect the AAF organization."[20] All those in positions of high command dealt daily with organization, reorganization, and all the administrative complexities included in the process.

According to Doolittle, the Northwest African Air Forces and the Twelfth Air Force had contributed in three major ways to Allied victory in North Africa. First, air superiority had been achieved over the African mainland. Second, Axis supplies had been reduced by successful interdiction campaigns. Third, as the campaign progressed, more and more support was rendered to the ground troops, which further enabled their success in the land battle. In spite of the difficulties, Jimmy's forces had achieved a great deal by the summer of 1943.

Eisenhower recognized Jimmy's success and his ability to learn from his mistakes. In a particularly telling letter, Eisenhower wrote, "When you joined me last year in London, you had much of what it takes to exercise high command; but I am not exaggerating in any sense when I tell you that in my opinion you have shown the greatest degree of improvement of any of the senior United States officers in my command. You have become a soldier in every sense of the word and you are, every day, rendering services of inestimable value to our country and to the United Nations."[21] Doolittle had matured and was developing into his rank while a commander in North Africa.

As fall approached, the Twelfth began flying strategic bombing missions—as opposed to interdiction—against the German homeland. By early October, the NASAF's Twelfth Air Force heavy bombers were transferred to Foggia, Italy, where they assumed the purely strategic mission of bombing targets in southern Germany and the Balkans. Doolittle was assigned as the commander of that force.

The question of whether or not to pursue the objectives of the Combined Bomber Offensive (CBO), as established during the Casablanca Conference in mid-January, from both England and Italy was hotly contested by American and British air leaders. Lt. Gen. Ira C. Eaker, Eighth Air Force Commander, along with Air Vice Marshal Sir Peter Portal, and Air Chief Marshal Sir Arthur Harris, feared that the buildup of a new strategic air force would cripple the CBO and jeopardize Overlord, the invasion of Europe. Doolittle, on the other hand, maintained that for accomplishing high-altitude bombardment of southern and eastern Germany and the Balkans during the upcoming winter, Foggia would provide approximately twenty more days of good bombing weather than England would. He argued his point by citing historical weather data for both regions. On 1 November 1943, the Fifteenth Air Force was activated and Doolittle took command. Both Spaatz and Arnold supported the plan that Doolittle had enunciated.[22]

The new Fifteenth Air Force consisted of nearly a thousand airplanes and twenty thousand men; many were simply transferred from the Twelfth Air Force. In eighteen months, Jimmy

Doolittle had jumped from lieutenant colonel to major general and held command of one of the largest strategic air arms in history. In this capacity, Jimmy had four major objectives: first, to destroy German air forces wherever they were found; second, to contribute when able to Operation Pointblank, the Allied operation against aircraft plants, ball bearing factories, petroleum plants, sub pens, and airfields; third, to support ground forces; and fourth, to attack and weaken German positions in the Balkans. Initial success was met by deteriorating weather during November and December, and fewer than ten missions were flown during those weeks.[23] Every commander in Europe, at one time or another, decried the weather as the greatest enemy of precision bombardment and mission accomplishment by American bomber crews.

The tempo of the war was accelerating rapidly, and Doolittle was about to be swept up by another turn of military plans. In December 1943, Eisenhower handpicked "Tooey" Spaatz as commander of U.S. Strategic Forces in Europe in preparation for the cross-channel invasion scheduled for summer 1944. This placed Spaatz in overall command of the Eighth and Fifteenth Air Forces. Doolittle, having earned the respect of all the major command players, was selected to replace Eaker as commander of the Eighth Air Force.

Eaker had vocally opposed the establishment of the Fifteenth Air Force, claiming that too many strategic resources were being spread too thin to launch effective attacks against the Germans. There were also other subtle differences in opinion between Eaker's command philosophy and Arnold's intent for Eaker's forces. Ralph H. Nutter, onetime command navigator for LeMay, wrote:

> He [Eaker] not only didn't get enough planes and bomb tonnage on targets, he didn't involve himself in the tactical planning and execution of the missions. . . . LeMay had questioned the purpose and value of the diversion to Regensburg and shuttle to North Africa. In approving it, Eaker had ignored LeMay's criticism and blessed a plan that cut the bomb tonnage on Schweinfurt in half. Eaker had

to know that with less than two hundred planes bombing Schweinfurt, they could not destroy the targets. . . . Arnold knew that Eaker
did not support his intention to bomb Germany to a pulp. Eaker
wanted the fighters to defend the bombers rather than use proactive
tactics against the Luftwaffe. Instead of having his fighters go after
the German fighters, Eaker instructed them to stay close and protect the bombers.[24]

Eaker's opposition to the Fifteenth and his restrictions on
his fighters may have contributed to Arnold's final decision to
reassign him from England to command the Mediterranean
Allied Air Forces (MAAF). Arnold recognized that the coming
spring was the last chance to achieve air supremacy before
Overlord. Highly capable but not overly aggressive with his
forces, Eaker possessed the rank and experience needed to run
the Italy-based strategic air forces, soon to grow by at least a
dozen heavy-bombardment groups. His diplomatic ability
would help to mold the multinational coalition of air forces
into the overall Mediterranean contribution to Overlord and
winning the war against the Axis.[25] Eaker never considered this
move a positive one.

The historical debate on Arnold's ultimate purpose in moving
Eaker has never been clearly determined. There is circumstantial
evidence, however, that Doolittle's understanding of Arnold's in-
tentions to destroy the Luftwaffe at all costs, versus Eaker's re-
luctance to allow his fighters to attack Luftwaffe fighters directly,
weighed heavily on the decision to transfer Eaker to the
Mediterranean. In Arnold's mind, Eaker had not delivered the
desired results and the CBO did not yet have air superiority over
Germany. Never mind that Eaker did not have long-range escort
capability or the growing numbers of strategic bombers that
Doolittle would eventually command.

In addition, Eaker was probably not thrilled with the idea of
being replaced by an old nemesis of his. Although a friendly yet
somewhat competitive relationship had existed since Doolittle
beat Eaker to Cleveland in the 1931 Thompson race, Eaker always seemed a second fiddle to Doolittle's accomplishments. For

instance, Eaker had continued Jimmy's pioneering instrument work by flying cross-country on instruments, but Doolittle had already claimed the publicity of the first blind landing. Most important, Eaker had designed the European daylight-bombardment campaign; he fought for it at Casablanca, and now Doolittle would carry it out.

The reality of Doolittle's promotion to commander of the Eighth Air Force is complicated but, in the big picture of the air war, was not meant as a demotion for Eaker. As a direct result of the conference at Sextant (code name for Cairo) during the first week in December 1943, it was decided that General Eisenhower rather than Gen. George Marshall would command the Overlord invasion of Europe. What resulted from this decision was the predictable toppling of the house of cards that welded the British and American military command structure tenuously together. Eisenhower moved from Supreme Command in the Mediterranean to Supreme Command in London. Politics then dictated that a British officer replace Eisenhower as ground commander in the Mediterranean. To balance the Mediterranean team, an American airman of sufficient rank and experience was required to act as the Mediterranean air commander. Since Eisenhower selected Spaatz to lead the overall air effort for D day, the only officer who had the requisite rank and experience was Ira Eaker.

Spaatz's 21 December memo to Eaker explained the situation in clear terms: "Because of close relationship with other services and other nationalities in both theaters and for most effective integration of effort I consider it essential that American air rank and experience be distributed between two theaters. Believe that command of an air force is of relatively less importance compared to overall requirements."[26] Additionally, Spaatz believed that the reorganized Eighth Air Force would function more as a bomber command rather than an entire air force. Moving Eaker was Spaatz's recommendation, since he was to remain in London with Ike. Had Eisenhower been ambivalent about his air commander, Eaker might have remained in London. Had Marshall rather than Eisenhower been selected to command Overlord, Eaker would definitely have remained in England. In the end, Spaatz suggested the choices, Arnold supported him, Eisenhower approved the moves, and Marshall "blessed" those recommendations.[27] The deal was done, and, essentially, Doolittle had not been involved in the process.

"The Mighty Eighth" was the most visible, most prestigious command in the Army Air Forces. In December 1943, Doolittle's newest command numbered 4,200 aircraft and more than 150,000 personnel. By June 1944, his personnel would more than double. As it was, Doolittle had inherited an Air Force still reeling from dismal defeats over targets in Ploesti, Regensberg, and Schweinfurt from August through October. The long-range P-51 had not then been available, and the raids had resulted in near-backbreaking losses. The Eighth was licking gaping wounds.

While the Eighth was recovering from the disastrous raids, no deep penetrations into Germany were attempted. Planes were built, shipped, and delivered to the Eighth Air Force in astonishing numbers—more than enough to replace previous losses. These included the new P-51 Mustang capable of escorting bomber formations all the way into Germany and back again.

On 27 December 1943, Gen. Hap Arnold, having just revamped the command structure of the European air forces, published one of the most important air orders of the war. In it, he summarized the situation in Europe and established the number one priority for Doolittle's command in 1944.

Arnold noted that American aircraft factories were turning out large quantities of airplanes, engines, and accessories and that training establishments were operating twenty-four hours a day, seven days a week, training crews. Further, he emphasized that enough aircraft and crews had been provided to cover unit attrition.

General Arnold based his primary air orders on a conceded fact: that Operation Overlord, the invasion of Europe, would not be possible unless the German air force was destroyed. The order read, "Therefore, my personal message to you—this is a

MUST—is to destroy the enemy air force wherever you find them, in the air, on the ground and in the factories."[28]

The last clause of this field order clearly delineated what Doolittle already knew and Eaker had never embraced. With this order, Jimmy and the Eighth Air Force set out to destroy the Luftwaffe, once and for all.

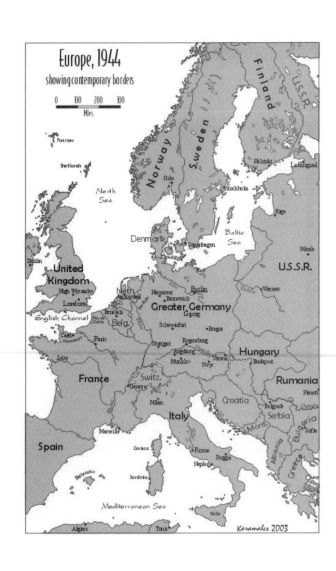

Europe, 1944

showing contemporary borders

0   100   200   300
        Miles

Faeroes

Shetlands

North
Sea

Norway

Sweden

Finland

U.S.S.R.

Oslo

Stockholm

Helsinki

Leningrad

Riga

Denmark

Copenhagen

Baltic
Sea

Minsk

Dublin

United
Kingdom

High Wycombe

London

English Channel

Caen
Normandy

Paris

Loire

Neth.
Amsterdam

Hanover
Brunswick

Berlin

Greater Germany

Leipzig

Schweinfut

Prague

Warsaw

U.S.S.R.

Pas de
Calais

Brussels

Belg.

Stuttgart

Regensburg

Augsburg

Munich

Steyr

Vienna

Budapest

Hungary

France

Switz.

Geneva

Milan

Croatia

Belgrade

Serbia

Rumania

Ploesti

Spain

Marseille

Corsica

Rome

Foggia

Naples

Italy

Mont.

Albania

Bulgaria

Sofia

Greece

Balearics

Sardinia

Mediterranean Sea

Sicily

Algiers

Tunis

Karamales 2003

Chapter 7

World War II: The Mature General

Major general doolittle transferred command of the Fifteenth Air Force to Brig. Gen. Nathan F. Twining on 3 January 1944. On the 6th, he officially took command of the Eighth and moved to his new headquarters at High Wycombe, in Buckinghamshire, England. His command consisted of an expanding twenty-five heavy-bomber groups and fifteen fighter groups. Additionally, the Ninth Air Force provided up to eighteen fighter groups for bomber escort when Spaatz thought it critical enough. Jimmy's responsibilities had become awesome. When he moved to High Wycombe, he became one of the few officers who, by January 1944, had served in all of America's major wartime theaters: the Pacific, the Mediterranean, Great Britain (northern Europe), and Washington D.C.[1]

Arnold's direct orders to Doolittle having been made clear, Jimmy went to work immediately. While taking the perfunctory tour of his command, he met with Maj. Gen. William E. "Bill" Kepner, who was in charge of the Eighth Fighter Command.

Prominently hung on Kepner's office wall was a sign that read, "The first duty of the Eighth Fighter Command is to bring the bombers back alive." Kepner had argued against being strictly tied to the bombers for many months, but Eaker and even Spaatz had insisted upon such a philosophy. Doolittle ordered Kepner to remove "that damned sign" and replace it with one that said, "The first duty of the Eighth Air Force fighters is to destroy German fighters." Kepner, thankful beyond words, unleashed his fighters in an offensive role.[2]

On 21 January, Jimmy announced the change in fighter doctrine to all his commanders. P-47s and P-38s with drop tanks and the arrival of the Merlin-powered P-51 Mustang extended the range of escort fighters all the way to Berlin. With this capability, one that Eaker never enjoyed, Doolittle felt confident that offensive air operations were not only possible but also essential. Fighters, he stated, "should be encouraged to meet the enemy and destroy him rather than be content to keep him away."[3] It was Doolittle's first significant change in operational orders for his command, and it signaled a swift change in philosophy that, in a few short months, would make major progress toward achieving Arnold's directive. As soon as there were "enough fighters," Jimmy ordered the doctrine of "ultimate pursuit," and he considered it the most important and effective military decision he made during the war.[4] It was a timely decision that was precipitated by the December 1943 shuffling of air bosses throughout AAF commands in Europe.

Initially, Doolittle's forces continued to suffer heavy losses. "We had in the early days [January and February]," Doolittle said, "a very difficult time making deep penetrations with heavy bombers. They were able to fight off some of the fighters with their own guns, but the Germans then began to develop rockets, and the German fighters would then stay outside of range of the bombers and lob rockets at them. So the bombers had no way of defending themselves."[5] During these months, most of the attacks were flown in poor weather and bombs were dropped with the aid of an American clone of the British H2S self-contained radar mapping set, called the H2X. Just before Jimmy's arrival, Eaker launched his largest single raid of the war—seven hundred aircraft were launched with P-38 and P-51 fighter cover. This raid, Eaker's last as commander of the Eighth, contributed to the largest tonnage of American bombs dropped during any month of the war up to that time—more than thirteen thousand tons.[6]

A word on the state of American bombing doctrine seems to be in order at this point. Clearly, the AAF entered the Second World War espousing the doctrine of daylight, precision bombardment. This was taught at the Air Corps Tactical School by a small cadre of officers and had permeated most, but not all, of the operational command ranks by the early 1940s. The realities of poor weather, inadequate numbers of aircraft of the proper type, technology shortfalls, and the dispersal of enemy industrial and military targets, particularly by 1944, forced a modification in the doctrine developed in the laboratory environment of Maxwell Field classrooms. The fact is that the AAF conveniently flowed back and forth between attempts at daylight precision and poor weather and night area bombardment, not only in Europe but also over Japan, from the fall of 1943 until the end of the war. Additionally, American planners clearly and openly supported RAF night area bombardment even before Casablanca and then participated in a planned twenty-four-hour-a-day campaign that depended upon area bombing to achieve major Casablanca objectives. On Jan. 21, 1943, the Combined Chiefs formalized the Casablanca Directive, establishing the Combined Bomber Offensive (CBO). Addressed to Eighth Air Force and RAF Bomber Command, the primary objectives of the bomber offensive were to destroy the German military industrial and economic system, and undermine the morale of the German people to a point where their armed resistance would be fatally weakened. The Army Air Forces were to eliminate the industrial and economic systems while the RAF program was geared toward reducing morale. Further, the AAF continued to experiment with new bombardment techniques (H2X) and area weapons (Aphrodite) that flew directly in the face of any claims of precision. On several occasions, secondary targets were specifically designed to cover areas rather than precision military or industrial sites. This apparent flexibility and adaptability to the realities of bombardment and its difficulties in 1944 opened the floodgates for massive raids over vast expanses of German territory and criticism over ethical and moral issues raised by nonprecision area bombardment. Doolittle was far less restricted in his operations than Eaker had been in the previous months.[7]

It is with this evolutionary bombing philosophy that the Eighth Air Force began operations in 1944. By February, Doolittle's forces would fracture the Luftwaffe's dominance in the air and begin the shift in momentum over Germany. Spaatz and his deputy, Maj. Gen. Frederick L. Anderson, Doolittle from the Eighth, Twining from the Fifteenth, and Eaker from the MAAF planned and ordered the missions that were flown in February against Germany under the code name Argument—massive attacks against the Luftwaffe and the German aircraft industry. This operation became known as Big Week.

Just as it had been an Arnold directive that spurred Jimmy to modify his fighter's doctrine from one of close defense of the bombers to one of direct offensive action against enemy fighters, it was another Arnold message that spurred Spaatz to launch Operation Argument. With the operation already planned and "in the can," commanders awaited the arrival of enough bombers and escort fighters and a week of good weather to order the operation. Arnold had inquired of Spaatz, "Can't we someday, and not too far distant, send out a big number—and I mean a big number—of bombers to hit something in the nature of an aircraft factory and lay it flat?"[8] As with most of Arnold's "suggestions," this was more like an order. He followed this suggestion by directing an all-out aerial assault on Germany that, despite the fact that he expected heavier than normal losses, was to be completed by 1 March 1944.[9] There was simply no time remaining to dillydally before Allied troops were expected to hit the beaches at Normandy. By mid-February, there were enough bombers and enough escort fighters, but the weather remained untenable. Army meteorologists then delivered the weather forecast for 20 February—an extended period of weather suitable for visual bombardment.

Spaatz, after weighing the concerns expressed by his fighter forces over icing conditions, personally issued the order to begin the raids. Doolittle's Eighth Air Force contributed the majority of the force on this first thousand-plus-bomber mission, accompanied by more than nine hundred fighters, over Axis territory. Technically, only 971 of the bombers received mission credit, but more than 1,000 were launched. Sixteen bomber wings, seventeen fighter groups, and sixteen RAF fighter squadrons packed the skies over Europe. Six of the bomber wings flew unescorted to Poland on a northern route while the rest attacked industrial targets around Leipzig and Brunswick in central Germany. Twelve targets that were involved in the manufacture of the component parts for Me-109s, Me-110s, Ju-88s, Ju-188s, and FW-190s were bombed. Damage was heavy in many target areas, but machine tools used in aircraft construction escaped significant destruction. Only twenty-one bombers were lost while damage to the targets was moderate—although the extent of the damage was not known in detail until after the war. This raid had been preceded by an RAF night attack on Leipzig and would be followed each night by coordinated RAF night area bombing raids upon targets that complemented the combined forces' bombing scheme.[10]

Similar raids were flown on the 21st and 22d with somewhat less success. On the 23d, the entire Eighth Air Force was grounded due to unforecast low clouds and icing conditions while the Fifteenth flew only 102 bombers against ball-bearing factories in Steyr, Austria. On Thursday and Friday, the clouds broke and once again massive attacks upon Germany were launched. More than eight hundred bombers of the Eighth and Fifteenth Air Forces attacked Augsburg, Stuttgart, Schweinfurt, and Regensburg under clear skies, suffering modest losses. Damage inflicted during these raids was severe and largely the result of a precision visual attack. When the aircraft landed after these missions, Big Week officially came to an end.[11]

During Argument, the USSTAF and the RAF had pummeled the German homeland with radar and visual bombing missions. Losses were high but fewer than originally predicted by many commanders, including Doolittle. Of the 3,800 bombers that flew during the week, the Eighth lost 158, the Fifteenth lost 89, and more than 2,600 airmen were killed, wounded, or captured. Roughly ten thousand tons of bombs were dropped by American forces, which equaled the total tonnage dropped by the Eighth Air Force during its entire first year of operations. The RAF attacks against five German cities were equally massive. More than 2,300 bombers dropped nearly ten thousand tons of bombs while losing 157 aircraft that week.

Despite the remarkable tonnage unleashed, the effects upon German industry were (and still are) difficult to assess precisely. Perhaps the most accurate conclusion concerning the impact of these raids is the fact that "the Germans suffered only a temporary setback in their overall program of aircraft production is less important than that they lost a significant number of planes at a critical point in the air war and that, at the same critical juncture, they were forced to reorganize and disperse the entire industry."[12] Of greater impact than the material attacks upon industrial targets was the fact that the Luftwaffe came up to meet the bombers and was shot out of the sky in large numbers. Its losses of fighters and pilots would continue into March and, by April, resulted in the inability to combat the Allied air offensive. By the end of February, the Eighth had lost three hundred bombers. The Luftwaffe, however, had sacrificed one third of its single-engine fighters and nearly 20 percent of its fighter pilots.[13]

Big Week signaled a transformation of the air campaign against Germany. It was the first time that the AAF had launched one thousand bombers on any single raid—a force size approaching the one that Air Chief Marshal Sir Arthur "Bomber" Harris, commander in chief of Bomber Command, had advocated for many months. It was also during this week that the overall strength of the Eighth Air Force surpassed that of RAF Bomber Command. For all the squabbling that had occurred over air doctrine and command of air forces during the first two years of the air campaign, American airmen, in large measure, assumed greater control of the air war after Big Week's conclusion.[14]

What did Jimmy Doolittle think of the February attacks? "What hurt the Germans the most was the deterioration of the experience level of their pilots. . . . they lost about 1000 pilots between January and April. . . . The rate of attrition of the Luftwaffe's pilots exceeded Germany's rate of replacement. Also, the several months of reduced aircraft production during a crucial period created a temporary shortage of reserve aircraft that was difficult to overcome. Thus, Germany was low on two essentials at a critical point: aircraft and pilots."[15] Because of this, the Eighth Air Force enjoyed increasing, although not complete, air superiority over the Luftwaffe during the remainder of the war.

At the personal level, there was one significant change in Doolittle's Eighth Air Force command policies from his previous command duties. He no longer flew combat missions. Having knowledge of the Ultra code-breaking system and Operation Overlord, the upcoming D day invasion, he was forbidden from flying on any missions on which he might become an enemy prisoner of war. Secrecy was essential to the success of the invasion plan. Although he sometimes flew from base to base in Britain, he did so only over friendly territory and only rarely.[16] On one occasion he asked Spaatz for an exception to that policy—the first Eighth Air Force raid over Berlin. Had he led the mission as he had planned, he would have been the only pilot to bomb all three Axis capitals. In the end, Tooey changed his mind and Jimmy stayed on the ground. The first Berlin raid, flown on 4 March, was a complete fiasco, and two days later, 80 planes were lost out of a combined force of 660. The Luftwaffe was being squeezed back toward its capital and, despite often fierce and effective resistance, would soon be defeated over Berlin as it had been elsewhere. In fact, one of the major objectives of the Berlin raids was to draw the German fighters into the air and destroy them. The air war of attrition was clearly being won.[17]

During the remaining months of spring, Allied bombers continued to attack Pointblank targets in an effort to achieve Casablanca objectives. Pointblank was the name of the air operation intended to gain and maintain air superiority over the landing beaches in France. As all now recognized, and as was clearly written in AAF Manual 100–20 (1943), gaining air superiority was the first requisite, and thus the first priority, to successful daylight bombardment. Doolittle's orders for "ultimate pursuit" helped to achieve air superiority over most of Europe. "The long-range fighters were able to follow the bombers in," Doolittle stated, "and the fighters not only shot down the German aircraft in the air, but made a practice of coming back on the deck and shooting them up on the ground. So about that time we were doing real well and losses were getting very low due to the fact that our long-range fighters had pretty well taken over the air from the German fighters."[18]

The CBO officially ended on 1 April 1944, and the transfer of all air forces to Eisenhower took effect two weeks later. From that point on, the Allies began the systematic attack of targets in preparation for the Normandy invasion that summer. From Hanover to Berlin and south to Leipzig, along the Baltic coast, the Ruhr, over Munich, and the German V-1 rocket sites along the Pas de Calais, the Eighth continued to destroy industrial and military targets. In accomplishing these missions, a variety of bombardment techniques were used. Traditional high-altitude, precision, daylight attacks were still the means of choice, but radar bombing allowed attacks on industrial areas even when the weather was poor.

To assist in the accomplishment of these missions, the Eighth developed a plan to send long-range fighters out well in advance of the bomber forces. Devised by Col. Bud Peasley, these missions radioed back to the bombers the best route to the target, the best target weather, and other important flight information that only an on-station observer could provide. Organizing and authorizing "Air Scouts" was one of Doolittle's innovative contributions to the air war.[19]

A variation on this theme was the development of high-altitude bombing raids accomplished by fighter planes. Several P-38 Lightning fighters were modified to include a Norden bombsight in the nose, resulting in the nickname "Droop Snoot." Because of limited range, these planes bombed only targets near England, usually on the French coast. Another attempt was made to tighten bombing patterns by using P-47s flying in close formation to drop bombs on the command of a B-24 lead aircraft. In theory, the bombs would cluster closer together than if they were dropped from several wide-winged bombers in formation. These methods achieved uneven success and were limited due to the dire need for escort fighter protection.[20]

Clearly, the most experimental of these techniques was a project known as Aphrodite. Two different types of weapons, a series of glide bombs and remote-controlled nitro-starch-filled, war-weary bombers remotely piloted from a trailing mother ship, were used during this operation. Aphrodite was an attempt to protect airmen from deadly flak belts over high-value targets. The glide bombs, capable of gliding one mile for each thousand feet of altitude, were initially unguided and not very accurate, with a computed error of up to one mile around the target. Bombers used radio-controlled steering and aimed by using a television camera mounted on the bomb to direct later models. This method, of course, depended on visual conditions if a pinpoint strike was desired. These standard one-thousand- or two-thousand-pound bombs affixed with a small set of wings were employed by the Eighth from mid-1943 until May 1944.

Immediately after the GB series was shelved due to ridiculous inaccuracy, the radio-controlled "Weary Willy" contrivance took to the skies. In essence, each orphan B-17 or PB4Y (a naval B-24) was packed full with twenty thousand pounds of TNT (nitro-starch). The pilot took off and flew the plane to the English Channel, the bombardier armed the explosives, and the two crewmen parachuted out of a large hole cut in the bottom of the bomber's fuselage. These monstrous "bombs" were originally planned for use against submarine pens and V-1 and V-2 missile sites. A few blew themselves out of the sky when the explosives went off prematurely. About a dozen were guided across the channel and detonated near targets in France, inflicting little damage but creating huge holes in the ground. Aphrodite, a concept well ahead of the technology of the day, was shelved when the British began to fear reprisals by V-2 rockets as a result of errant Aphrodite attacks.[21]

The purpose behind this brief examination of these failed programs is simply to demonstrate that the AAF, from Arnold to Spaatz to LeMay and Doolittle, had accepted the fact that precision daylight bombing was not the only way to attack enemies from the air. Clearly, the purpose of several of these projects was to deliver weapons to targets while increasing the survival potential for airmen. Successful, accurate employment of such "standoff" weapons would not be possible for nearly five decades.[22]

While Doolittle's bombers expanded their targets to transportation and petroleum in the ensuing months, their mission focus was sharpened in preparation for the upcoming Overlord landings. Doolittle stated that there were four specific goals for the Eighth Air Force. First, attacks upon the aircraft industry and the Luftwaffe continued. Second, the destruction of enemy transportation targets located in northern France, the Low Countries, and western Germany was elevated in priority. Third, coastal targets from V-weapon sites to coastal defense batteries were selected specifically to soften defenses around the beaches. Finally, all airfields within 130 miles of Caen were to be reduced to unusable status. This perpetuated the ruse that the landing would occur there rather than more to the south as planned. Fighters roamed the railways seeking opportune targets and destroyed them at will.[23] By the 6th of June, it had become clear that German aerial resistance would be extremely limited during the landings at Normandy.

As testimonial to General Eisenhower's confidence in the successful outcome of the air battle, he felt comfortable massing his invasion forces in the open, a doctrinal violation that even his newly graduated West Point son, visiting his father in England, thought appalling. Eisenhower reassured young John that "if I didn't have air supremacy, I wouldn't be here."[24] Although that confidence was well founded, the price paid in the skies over Europe was great and there remained a balance due.

Early on the morning of the invasion, postponed a few days because of bad weather, Doolittle and his deputy, Maj. Gen. Earl E. "Pat" Partridge, each hopped into a P-38 and toured the landing zones. Doolittle witnessed landing craft attempting to reach the beaches at the Omaha landing area suffering heavy casualties. Many were destroyed before the troops could debark. Doolittle reported his observations directly to Eisenhower at the morning staff meeting, a report that "beat [Ike's] official intelligence report by several hours."[25] By the next morning, all landing forces had established beachheads in France. The breakout, still a few weeks away, would reveal other weaknesses in American bombardment doctrine and in the coordination between ground and air forces that resulted in hundreds of casualties from friendly fire.

The worst of these occurred during the last week in July. Heavy and medium bombers had targeted enemy front lines near the Thirtieth Infantry Division's lines. Malfunctioning equipment and poor decisions by bombardiers flung tons of high-explosive and fragmentary bombs into American positions—and this occurred several days in a row. More than a hundred American soldiers were killed, including Lt. Gen. Lesley J. McNair, and nearly four hundred were wounded. To place this in a modern-day perspective, in this operation alone, these friendly-fire casualties were roughly equal to the total number of casualties suffered by the entire multinational force that repatriated Kuwait during Desert Storm in 1991—approximately five hundred total casualties including just over a hundred killed by enemy fire.[26]

Much to Doolittle's surprise, orders continued to dictate close bombardment, this despite continued incidents of fratricide.

Eisenhowertried to lessen the tremendous guilt that Jimmy was feeling over these continued events. On 2 August, Eisenhower wrote, "I know how badly you and your command have felt because of the accidental bombing of some of our own troops. . . . Nevertheless, it is quite important that you do not give the incident an exaggerated place in your mind or in your future planning. . . . I want you and your command to know that the advantages resulting from the bombardment were of inestimable value."[27] Efforts were already well under way to remedy the problems that had resulted in the fatal bombing errors. Eisenhower's acceptance of these casualties demonstrated that he understood the technology of the day was inherently inaccurate and using it required the acceptance of risk.

Other obstacles appeared in the air during 1944. German jet and rocket planes concerned Jimmy when they appeared in the fall of 1944. The Me-262 demonstrated speed far superior to any aircraft in the air at that time. German head-on and perpendicular attack tactics caused problems and resulted in moderate losses for the bomber forces. Normally, however, the jet pilots simply flew fast and out of range of ever present fighter escorts. Coincidentally, Hitler modified the employment scheme for the jets and the pressure was eliminated until the spring of 1945, when it was too late. To counter such sporadic attacks, bombing and strafing of the jet bases occasionally applied pressure so that the Me-262 and other fighters could not attack Allied bombers in large, coordinated attack formations.[28]

In June 1944, German employment of unmanned jet bombs (V-1) and ballistic missiles (V-2) to attack cities in England also forced a reaction by the Allies. Operation Crossbow targeted the launch and production facilities for these weapons. Reacting to such attacks, the Eighth Air Force targeted V-1 and V-2 sites occasionally and without much enthusiasm. Doolittle clearly placed the transportation plan above Crossbow targets on his priority list. In one exchange between Doolittle and Eisenhower's deputy, Air Chief Marshal Sir Arthur Tedder, Jimmy explained that he had not followed an earlier directive to bomb Crossbow sites because targets in central Germany, as well as the destruction of bridges and railroads, were far more important than unmanned missile sites.[29] Tedder did not agree, nor did the citizens of London.

Despite these relatively minor distractions, the Eighth Air Force fell into a deadly routine of briefing, bombing, debriefing, and recovering. The air effort had become a mechanical process of destruction and further destruction. Doolittle worried less about his airmen while they were airborne and began to concentrate more on morale while they were on the ground. Parties were held, entertainment was provided, and promotions and medals were conferred. Meanwhile, Doolittle had occasion to meet with both Prime Minister Winston Churchill, one of the most brilliant men Jimmy said he had ever met, and King George VI.[30]

As testimony to the continuing air war over Europe after D day is the following statistic. Approximately half of the total bomb tonnage dropped on Axis targets was dropped *after* 6 June 1944.[31] It was also a tribute to the resiliency of the Luftwaffe that by November 1944, fighter attacks against Allied bomber formations had increased from the month before. Since aircraft production in Germany had not been severely disrupted (the country produced more than four thousand fighters in September alone), the Luftwaffe had plenty of planes. In a somewhat surprising move, the Germans stopped flying bombardment aircraft and transferred all their pilots to fighters. This left the Werhmacht virtually unprotected. All fighters were ordered to intercept the Allied bombers. On 27 and 28 September, for example, the Eighth lost sixty-four aircraft—no small tally considering that the Allies enjoyed air superiority. Yet these types of losses were relative compared to the tonnage of bombs being dispersed. It was actually a shortage of fuel and trained pilots that eventually kept the Germans on the ground.[32]

As target sets were reduced and tonnage was increased, cries of "terror bombing" began to surface. RAF bombers were leveling towns while AAF bombers continued to target factories and support facilities. Doolittle explained that "it is a fact in the grim business of strategic warfare that the results of such bombing efforts do not show up immediately on the battlefront. It is also a fact that when strategic targets are attacked, noncombatants will be killed. There is no way to hit factory buildings, railroad yards, and other such things without killing or maiming the civilians who are making the enemy's war materials."[33] In fact, this clearly reflects the accepted bombardment doctrine that Doolittle had directed as Eighth Air Force commander. Officially, precision bombing was considered synonymous with reduced civilian casualties. During the air campaign in 1944 and 1945, it was obvious that civilians were targets—indirectly in the case of the Allied daylight campaign and directly in the case of the RAF night area campaign. In Great Britain, the "whirlwind" wrought upon German cities was generally accepted as payback for Hitler's destruction of Europe and his direct attack on England.

As Churchill's England felt about Germany, FDR's America felt about Japan, and when the strategic air campaign in Europe was terminated on 16 April 1945, Doolittle anticipated a trip back to the States and a return to a more normal life. Instead, just after Churchill declared 8 May as V-E day, Arnold ordered Jimmy to redeploy his Eighth Air Force to Okinawa, where he would initiate strategic attacks against the Japanese mainland with the technically advanced B-29 Superfortress. Jimmy left England on 10 May 1945. He was on his way back to finish what his Raiders had started three years before.[34]

Chapter 8

War's End and After

JIMMY ARRIVED HOME in May and, after a second-honeymoon-like vacation in Miami with Joe, spent the summer on a West Coast public relations tour paired with Georgie Patton. Accompanied by their wives, the generals met in Denver, and the road show began. Doolittle recalled that Georgie, "replete with shiny steel helmet, ivory-handled pistol, large round belt buckle, highly polished boots, battle jacket, swagger stick, and jodhpurs, was a hit with the public and press photographers wherever he went."[1] Jimmy wore his summer uniform and "crushed" mission cap and looked just like any air officer. Their styles complemented each other nicely, and although Patton's language was sometimes controversial, the tour was a popular success.

Jimmy visited a few factories in California and spoke to Boeing employees in Seattle during an examination of the B-29 Superfortress that he was to command in the Pacific. It took a B-17, however, to get him there. An errant wind had blown a large piece of metal debris into the prop of the B-29 that was scheduled as his transport, grounding the craft. On 17 July 1945, Doolittle, representing the entirety of the Eighth Air Force, arrived on Okinawa beneath the shadow of the successful Trinity atomic bomb test carried out in the New Mexico desert that morning.[2] For the next two weeks, he began to organize his new command but his efforts turned out to be unnecessary.

After Maj. Charles W. Sweeney had dropped the second atomic weapon he was forced to land his B-29, *Bockscar,* on Okinawa to refuel. Due to poor weather over Japan, he had bombed his secondary target and did not have enough fuel to make his home base at Tinian. On Okinawa, Sweeney debriefed the mission in Doolittle's private office. Jimmy had become aware of the existence of the atomic bomb only after Col. Paul W. Tibbetts had dropped the first one on Hiroshima three days before. The culmination of the Manhattan Project provided a weapon that kept Doolittle's Pacific bombers from ever flying in combat.

Still, the war was not yet over. Just prior to the Japanese surrender, LeMay, on Arnold's orders, launched the last 1000-plus-plane raid of the war. Doolittle called it "a convincing finale to hostilities." Although given an opportunity to launch Eighth Air Force bombers against the Japanese, Doolittle declined to risk any plane or crew simply to receive a combat credit. The war ended when Emperor Hirohito announced the end of hostilities to his people via radio broadcast on 15 August.[3]

The surrender ceremony, presided over by Gen. Douglas MacArthur, took place on the deck of Admiral Halsey's flagship, the battleship *Missouri*, surrounded by 260 Allied warships, which had anchored in Tokyo Bay. Doolittle was one of many who witnessed the surrender ceremony while standing in military formation on the deck. He stood within sight of the very targets he and his Raiders had bombed three years earlier—then he was a lieutenant colonel, now a lieutenant general. After the signatures had dried, more than two thousand Army and Navy aircraft flew over the *Missouri*. The symbolic battleship, named after Truman's home state, flew the same flag that had flown above the Capitol on 7 December 1941. For the citizens of Tokyo, emotions varied from relief to humiliation and hatred. To all it meant the end of many bitter years of struggle.[4]

By 19 September, Jimmy was back in Washington, D.C., and was reunited with Joe and the boys. There, Alex Fraser, Doolittle's old boss at Shell, asked him to return to the company as a member of the board and a company vice president, an offer he accepted that December. When he began his terminal military leave in January, he immediately started his new job with Shell. He was to monitor the aviation side of the business and act as a senior adviser on all aviation projects. He reported only to his boss and friend, Fraser, and had no one to supervise—it was not a high-pressure job. His pay was triple what he had earned as a three-star general, and Shell provided him with a refurbished B-25 for travel and engine and fuel-oil testing.

Until 1963, Jimmy held civilian positions while concurrently serving on military and scientific committees such as the USAF Scientific Advisory Board and the National Advisory Committee for Aeronautics. His role in many of these groups—often supervisory—attached a renowned name to each group.

Before Jimmy got too involved in panels and committees, however, he had some personal business to accomplish concerning the whereabouts of his lost Raiders. The horrible truth about the execution of three of the Raiders had reached America in 1943. A fourth had succumbed to disease while imprisoned. The remaining four were held as prisoners until after the bomb fell on Nagasaki, on 9 August 1945.[5]

Although the end of the war finally revealed the Raiders' fates, it signaled only the beginning of the fighting among the Army, the Navy, and the Army Air Forces. The air forces' struggle to gain independence, certainly plausible after the excellent performance of the AAF in the air around the globe during the past four years, meant that assets, men, and money would be taken from established branches and used to create the independent air arm. Arnold asked Doolittle to visit several cities and inform the public about the concept of a unified defense department that included a separate and equal air force. From 1 October until nearly Christmas, Doolittle made eighteen speeches from New York to Los Angeles. He had taken up the mantle as Arnold's primary airpower advocate and, as such, believed that "an autonomous Air Force and a single Department of National Defense would eliminate useless duplication and waste. It would cut down the existent war-expanded defense organization and would tend to assure the equitable distribution of available funds according to actual military value. There would be more money spent on new, modern weapon systems, and no unnecessary airplanes, carriers, or battleships would be built."[6] The struggle that Doolittle articulated continues even today.

Following Arnold's lead, which was significantly different from the Navy's bulldozer approach, Doolittle tried to calm the waters being disturbed by that political machine. Before the Senate Military Affairs Committee, he testified that teamwork and cooperation between the services had won the war, not independent operations. Doolittle's experiences reflected this more directly than those of many other air commanders. The Tokyo raid included AAF planes launched by a naval task force. The D day operation was clearly a joint and combined service venture that not only included close coordination among land, sea, and air forces but also was commanded by an Army nonflying officer. By action rather than argument, the other services understood the importance of joint operations. The issue, as it usually is in Washington, was one of funding—rather, the threat of losing funding. Both the U.S. Army and the Navy recognized that a separate Air Force would cost them a sizable portion of their budgets.

On 1 January 1946, Jimmy left active service, but his affiliation with American airpower continued. Later that month, Jimmy became the first president of the Air Force Association (AFA), a nonprofit advocacy organization made up of AAF veterans. General Arnold selected Jimmy for much the same reason he had selected him to lead the Tokyo Raid. Arnold wrote, "Not only could he be counted upon to do a task himself if it were humanly possible, but he could impart his spirit to others."[7]

Arnold felt certain that with Jimmy in charge, the organization could not fail. "Your concern over more than a quarter of a century," Arnold said, "symbolizes the spirit of fellowship and continued interest in the Air Force traditions which this organization is pledged to perpetuate."[8] Doolittle, as the most famous AAF officer at war's end, was once again Arnold's "natural choice."

Not surprisingly, his first battle as AFA president was fought against the U.S. Navy and revolved around the creation of a unified Department of Defense. President Truman had tabled the unification issue in early 1946. This gave Air Force advocates time to make their case against a well-established and highly skilled naval advocacy machine. Doolittle, in a 24 July 1946 *New York Times* interview, hammered the Navy. He made it clear that naval advocates were confusing organization and operations: "I do not wish to impugn the Navy's motives. It is not whether the Navy and the Navy advocates are sincere in their expressed beliefs. It is that they are wrong."[9] Clearly, Jimmy *did* wish to impugn the Navy's motives, and he had no compunction about doing so, politely, as a retired AAF general.

He further impugned the Navy's motives when he testified at a hearing of the Senate Naval Affairs Committee that fall. Like the experienced boxer he was, he pulled no punches:

> The Navy has long considered that it represents the first line of defense for America. The air has now taken the role of the "first line of defense" from the sea. . . . Anyone capable of understanding, who is aware of even the most basic truths upon which World War II was prosecuted, is fully aware that the first line of defense and the last frontiers of America lie in the sky. . . . In the name of common sense, let the Navy go to sea and, if it wishes, carry its carrier-based aircraft with it; but by the same token, let it cease this under-handed effort to extend its role into the sphere of strategic bombardment. That sphere belongs to the Air Force. . . . The question before us is whether we shall produce and maintain at prohibitive costs and tremendous waste and duplication two separate and self-sufficient air forces. The alternative is a separate, unified, and streamlined Air Force whose command shall have power to range through the skies seeking the enemy wherever he may be, in whatever form. . . . What is good for the United States, as far as our armed forces are concerned, is that the activities of all services should be coordinated and each service should retain full control in its own medium and stay out of the others'

medium. . . . It might be well for the Navy to examine with detachment and candor the military future of this age of atomic bombs. Ten-thousand-mile bombers, rockets, and guided missiles, and accept for itself the possibility that science has rendered unnecessary the bulk of the Navy, which operates upon the surface of the sea.[10]

The gloves were off, and Jimmy, along with other Mitchell disciples, was fighting for the very existence of an independent U.S. Air Force.

How much his public efforts contributed to acceptance of the legislation that separated the Air Force from the Army cannot accurately be determined. For its part, however, Doolittle led the charge, in the AFA and by his congressional testimony. On 26 July 1947, President Truman signed the National Security Act into law. On 18 September, the Air Force officially became a separate service.[11] Although the notion of an independent USAF had been long advocated by Army air officers, the final establishment of an independent Air Force was clearly a major compromise—one that established the organization of the USAF but failed to achieve unification of air assets under that single organization. In a feature issue that fall, *Air Force*, the official journal of the AFA, stated: "No one pretends that the National Security Act is a panacea. It is a compromise and an experiment. Time will undoubtedly dictate many changes and amendments."[12]

Three days after that, Jimmy Doolittle flew his final flight as a pilot in command (PIC). It was fitting that his final PIC sortie was flown in Shell's B-25—representative of both his close association with civil aeronautical technology and his inexorable ties to AAF combat operations. During his thirty-year flying career, Jimmy logged more than ten thousand flight hours—meaning he spent more than one year of his life in the sky—and flew 265 different aircraft. These are almost unfathomable numbers for his day and still impressive to modern military and civilian pilots alike. He became too busy to fly sufficient hours to maintain his proficiency and, realizing that, simply quit.[13] It was decisions such as this one that allowed him to age into what some considered unlikely: an old, bold pilot.

Filling his schedule during 1946 until 1950, Doolittle served on a variety of committees and acted as a science and technology adviser to Gen. Hoyt S. Vandenberg, who took Spaatz's place as Air Force Chief of Staff in 1948. In that role, he was responsible for recommendations on how best to reorganize procurement and research functions within the Air Force. Gen. Bernard A. Schriever, the first chief of scientific liaison appointed by General Arnold, pointed out "Doolittle's influence was instrumental in gaining technology 'a seat at the table,' where the decisions were made about the Air Force's future force requirements. This was a monumental achievement, given the entrenched procurement authority of Wright Field's Air Materiel Command and the pressure from the short-term interests of the operators. More than anyone else, it was Jimmy Doolittle—with his across-the-board credibility—who led and won the battle for technology."[14] It was a battle Jimmy had begun during his earliest test-flying days.

Jimmy became associated with, although not yet a member of, the newly formed USAF Scientific Advisory Board (SAB) chaired by Dr. Theodore von Kármán, a brilliant theoretical aerodynamicist who had emigrated from Hungary during the rise of Fascism. Initially, he contributed to what became the first ad hoc committee fielded by the SAB. Led by Dr. Louis Ridenour, dean of the University of Illinois, this mix of SAB and civilian members established the model for future SAB study committees.

The Ridenour Committee met with General Vandenberg on 11 July 1949, and he charged them to "give us a picture of what we [the USAF] ought to be doing but what we are not doing."[15] For the next few months the committee toured a variety of Air Force installations and evaluated research practices. The recommendations made by that group—later also known as the Doolittle Committee—resulted in the establishment of a separate command organization within the USAF dedicated specifically to research and development activities. Additionally, one of the most significant recommendations in the report concerned the introduction of systems engineering. In the past, procurement of aircraft and the equipment that supported them was accomplished in sequential steps—aircraft first, then bombs, then electronics, then support equipment like bomb loaders. Systems engineering allowed for the construction of many components concurrently, thereby allowing the weapon system to become operational in less time. It was Doolittle's opinion that the adoption of systems engineering "was probably the one thing that brought our missile program into actual operational use as rapidly as possible."[16]

After the successful airlift of supplies to Berlin during 1948–49, the first hostile shots of the Cold War were fired on and around the Korean Peninsula in June 1950. Jimmy openly criticized the conduct of the air war over Korea. He twice went to Korea and reported back to General Vandenberg that the war was a stalemate and would remain so "as long as our Air Force could not attack the sources of manufacture and supply in China . . . [any] 'forceful action' had to be more than strikes against supply lines."[17] Doolittle advocated a bombardment doctrine similar to the one his bomber forces had practiced only five years earlier. The politicians forbade such deep attacks, and having two sons fighting that war, Jimmy continually advocated a strategic style of bombing that was never really accomplished in that theater.

By 1951, Jimmy had accepted the vice chairmanship of the SAB, often substituting for Kármán who traveled frequently as a member of several international aeronautical committees, a professor at Caltech, and the head of the Jet Propulsion Laboratory (JPL) in California. Doolittle assumed the chairmanship of the SAB in November 1955 and held that position until December 1958.

Additionally, Jimmy's committee association with the National Advisory Committee for Aeronautics (NACA) eventually resulted in his appointment as chairman in 1956. Until then, he had served on the NACA Main Committee and contributed to other subcommittees when needed. The reality of having one individual chair both the national civil aeronautics committee and one of the military's most influential aeronautics groups was unprecedented. This also reflected the national leadership's acceptance of Doolittle's credentials as a civilian scientist and businessman while demonstrating the trust held in him by the Air Force. No other man could have successfully served in both positions at once. No one else would have wanted to.

Historian Alex Roland, in his history of the NACA, adeptly described the uniqueness of Doolittle's appointment to the chair at the NACA:

> Any one of his careers would have occupied and fulfilled most men, but Doolittle managed them all and continued in 1956 to bring them a vitality and energy that belied his 60 years. . . . All Doolittle's credentials, however, could not change the fact that he stood tradition of the NACA chairmanship on its head. Save only the first incumbent [1915], all of the chairmen had been scientists, and all but one had been academics. . . . If Doolittle was anything, he was an academic last; first or second he was a businessman, second or first a military officer. He was the personification of what Eisenhower was soon to label the military-industrial complex.[18]

Today, as fields in the history of technology evolve, Doolittle is even more representative of the military-industrial-academic complex described in more recent literature as having roots before the Second World War began.

Doolittle's apparently endless supply of energy could not save the NACA from its demise after the USSR launched *Sputnik* in October 1957. Space flight had become a reality, and the NACA was not equipped to deal with both aeronautics and astronautics. In an attempt to remedy that shortfall, the National Aeronautics and Space Act was passed in July 1958. Less than one month later, the NACA held its final meeting. Doolittle realistically assessed the dissolution of the NACA: "While we [the NACA] knew that missiles would have a very important place, while we knew that space must be explored, we were hesitant to turn over to the missile people and their supporters all of the funds that we had been receiving for the development of the airplane and associated equipment. . . . In retrospect, I think we all agree that we were wrong."[19]

Jimmy knew that the NACA had failed to make the leap into space at the right time largely because of his association with the SAB. In 1953, Jimmy had persistently levied for the creation of a nuclear weapons panel as part of the SAB ad hoc committee system. On this panel, Dr. John von Neumann and Dr. Edward Teller eventually determined that a lightweight ("dry") nuclear warhead could be joined with a ballistic missile. The USAF and the Intercontinental Ballistic Missile (ICBM) force were the result of that realization, and Doolittle served as an adviser on most of the panels that reviewed ICBM development during the 1950s.[20] The ICBM, of course, developed into one of the triad of strategic weapons designed to counter the Soviet nuclear threat throughout the Cold War.

While many of his projects were directly related to military aviation and space studies, Jimmy concurrently served on a host of civil committees as well. In February 1952, in the aftermath of a series of fatal crashes in New Jersey, President Truman asked him to chair the President's Airport Commission to investigate and report upon the growing hazards associated with commercial flying in and around crowded cities. Truman, wanting a quick turnaround, asked that the ninety-day study objectively and realistically examine airport location and design. Working at the Department of Commerce, Doolittle; Charles F. Horne, head of the Civil Aeronautics Administration; and Jerome C. Hunsaker, chair of the NACA, went immediately to work.

During March, the three-man team interviewed aviation-safety experts and industrialists and traveled to sixteen busy airports for firsthand reports on their operations. Doolittle released the commission's critical report on 16 May 1952. In it, recommendations called for federal funding to remedy the deteriorating state of airports. Needed was more money for runway construction and air traffic control systems and laws that strictly governed the airport environment. As Truman's 1953 budget included a cut in airport funding, this report had little impact.

Eventually, some attention was given to the zoning-law issue, which resulted in clear areas underneath the approach and departure courses near airfields. Of course, these were dubbed "Doolittle zones."[21]

General Eisenhower's election to the presidency in 1952 afforded Doolittle more opportunities for government service. Logically, Doolittle was picked to head the fiftieth-anniversary celebration of the Wright's first powered flight. In 1954 Doolittle was asked to investigate the CIA. President Eisenhower was looking for an excuse to exert greater control over the increasingly independent attitudes developing there. Doolittle fingered CIA chief Allen Dulles for poor administrative ability, but Eisenhower did not act to reform the agency.[22] Perhaps related to all his travels, Doolittle concurrently served on Ike's Foreign Intelligence Advisory Board, another hush-hush group. Additionally, Doolittle became a member of the advisory board to the National Air and Space Museum. In this capacity, he lent his name to a Hall of Fame roster of aviators. The Smithsonian Institution over the years has benefited from the forethought of Hap Arnold and his followers, who in 1945 directed that one of every airplane should be collected and displayed in a national air museum.

Approaching mandatory retirement within the Shell organization, Jimmy prepared with Joe to move to the West Coast. In April 1958, while finishing up some Air Force business in Puerto Rico, Jimmy received crushing news from home. Jim Jr. was dead by his own hand.

"It does us no good to speculate why our firstborn took his irrevocable step. He left no clues and never discussed his personal feelings or problems with anyone in our family or with friends. . . . I can think of no greater misfortune for parents than when a child dies out of sequence in the natural order. It is something that I don't think one ever fully recovers from . . . [Joe and I] seldom talked about our loss, but we never got over it."[23] This tragic event marked the beginning of a significant change in Doolittle's working and personal life.

Chapter 9

California and Conclusions

A<small>LTHOUGH HE SERVED</small> on the Shell board of directors until the late 1960s, Jimmy officially retired as a working Shell employee in 1958. Never, however, did he intend to fully retire. The formation of a new company conceived by Dean Wooldridge and Simon Ramo, brilliant scientists, afforded Doolittle another opportunity. Funded by Thompson Products, TRW (Thompson-Ramo-Wooldridge) was formed with Doolittle as a member of the board of directors. Soon after the establishment of that company, driven by the expanding aerospace industry, they spun off a subsidiary firm, Space Technology Laboratories (STL). Jimmy accepted the chairmanship of STL, a delightful prospect because the company was located in Los Angeles. During January 1959, Jimmy and Joe had happily returned to Southern California.

Partly due to conflict-of-interest fears, and partly because he had too many obligations to successfully complete, Jimmy resigned from several committees and panels on which he had served during the 1950s. He also made it a point to hunt and fish more regularly than in previous years.

Jimmy, as many true hunters do, firmly believed in the principles of conservation of resources. He believed in the efficacy of game laws and followed them throughout his many years. He treasured being honored as the Winchester-Western Sportsman of the Year in 1974. The prize was a Winchester Super-X model-1 auto-loading shotgun—serial number 1-9-4-2. Jimmy seemed to appreciate the wonders of nature to a greater degree later in his life and spent several detailed pages in his autobiography explaining this philosophy. "It is a crime against nature," he wrote, "to have any animal or bird become extinct through the excesses and selfishness of people."[1] Jimmy's interests were broad. One Air Force historian very accurately labeled him a true "Renaissance man of aviation."[2] More accurately, Jimmy Doolittle was a Renaissance man of the twentieth century.

Jimmy enjoyed one luxury that most retired military generals did not—a long life. During the 1960s, Doolittle, politically neutral during his service years, actively supported and campaigned for Barry M. Goldwater (R., Arizona) as a presidential candidate. He and Clare Booth Luce cochaired the Citizens for Goldwater-Miller Committee, a fund-raising organization. Goldwater's conservative views reflected many of Jimmy's personal beliefs. Goldwater's forthrightness, one of the reasons he was not a popular candidate, was particularly satisfying to Doolittle, who, until that time, had diligently avoided any serious political involvement following his military career.[3]

After a chance meeting with V. J. Skutt, the chief operating officer of the Mutual of Omaha Insurance Company, Jimmy was offered an honorary position on the executive board. Jimmy was not ready to simply lend his name to a board list and stipulated that he would accept the position only if his service would "contribute in a meaningful and significant way to the protection, safety, and well-being of the American public." Skutt accepted the counterproposal, and Jimmy served actively on eight different corporate boards and traveled overseas to assist in the establishment of new international branches.[4]

When Jimmy turned 72 in 1968, he retired from the boards of

Shell and TRW but remained an active consultant to Mutual of Omaha. From then until his death in 1993, at the age of 96, Doolittle's life was one of much relaxation interspersed with the ongoing gathering of awards and honors consistent with a lifetime of achievements in a number of diverse and exciting fields of endeavor. Just a few of the most noteworthy of the accolades were induction into the Aviation Hall of Fame in 1967, receipt of the Sylvanus Thayer Award at West Point in 1983, and being pinned with a fourth star by President Ronald Reagan and Senator Barry Goldwater, the sponsor of the legislation promoting Doolittle, in June 1985.

On their seventy-first wedding anniversary, 24 December 1988, Joe succumbed to complications from a previous stroke. She and Jimmy are now buried together in the nation's most hallowed ground, Arlington National Cemetery.

After Joe died, Jimmy moved to Pebble Beach, where his son John and daughter-in-law Priscilla had built their dream home on a piece of land that Jimmy and Joe had given to them several years earlier. Doolittle garnered more awards during his last few years, the most significant presented in Washington in 1989. President George H. W. Bush, with wife Barbara by his side, awarded Jimmy the Presidential Medal of Freedom in another White House ceremony. To this day, Jimmy Doolittle is the only man to ever receive both the nation's highest military and civilian honors.

The Medal of Freedom was received with a heavy heart without Joe. Doolittle had always considered their meeting and marriage the luckiest part of his life. Jimmy and Joe were the greatest of couples. They suffered tremendous tragedy, service separations, and euphoric successes with style and guarded humility. Considering the dozens of close calls and courageous events that occurred during his nine decades on earth—and in the air—Joe, not Jimmy, might have been the lucky one.

He lived content in his own wing of John's Pebble Beach home until his death on 27 September 1993.

James Harold Doolittle is an American legend. His life was quintessentially American. He was, in the most honest sense, a citizen-soldier—neither a career military man nor a lifelong business executive but a unique blend of both. Additionally, he was a soldier-scholar whose aeronautical studies were essential to the development of military and commercial aviation.

His upbringing in frontier Alaska molded his character, determination, and adventurous spirit. It made him tough, confident, and sometimes impulsive. Jimmy's diminutive size as a youth was at the root of his uncommon courage. From the time he was old enough to swing a fist, he had been the underdog, but rarely the vanquished. These characteristics, which were sharpened over the years by mature judgment and careful logic, marked the man who flew into aviation history in air races, experimental cockpits, and aeronautical laboratories and over hostile territory around the world. Doolittle's journey into legend began on a rough country road and ended on a multilane superhighway.

There were many potholes along Doolittle's path to legend. He was nearly killed during early training flights and was directly involved in one accident that resulted in the death of a student pilot. Some of his mishaps resulted from mechanical failings that were common in the early years of flying. Others were the result of personal errors in judgment and flight discipline. All were costly. During his early flying career, he spent many days relegated to ground duties as a result of being caught violating military flying rules. He was in his early twenties and suffered from a lack of maturity and a desire to impress those around him.

Perhaps the most significant single stop along Doolittle's personal trip was his record-setting flight from Florida to California in 1922—the first transcontinental flight in less than twenty-four hours. The careful scrutiny of his military bosses and the aviation community and the ramifications of poor publicity required detailed preparations and practice for the mission. The initial "ground looping" failure of the flight was as important as its ultimate success on 5 September. The experience humbled Doolittle and forced him to recognize the high stakes involved in any type of miscalculation during such an adventure. At the age of twenty-five, he had taken a significant step toward growing up, both personally and as an aviator. Every one of his accomplishments after that, whether civilian or military, was the result of calculation, preparation, and assessment of the risks inherent to each event. Before this, Jimmy had been lucky in the air. After the completion of this historic flight, he made his own luck.

The years he spent in the commercial world at Shell taught him the realities of business in America. He was an effective salesman and contributed the knowledge and initiative that eventually led to the development and production of high-octane aviation fuel, a World War II essential for aircraft performance. His personal situation, one that required him to care for his ailing mother and mother-in-law, provided the impetus for his early departure from Army ranks. His civilian experiences, such as his membership on the 1934 Baker Board, were never too far away from important military contacts. In 1940, Doolittle, a major in the Army Specialists Reserve, was welcomed back into an Army officer corps that was then dominated by West Pointers. He became the only "nonregular" officer to command major combat air forces during the Second World War.

As Doolittle had taken several years to mature as a pilot, his elevation to command during World War II also required a growing-up process. Where Jimmy may have been a naturally gifted flyer, he required focus and specific goals to lift him to greatness in the sky. Command was no different, and the maturation process began when he was selected to lead the first American air raid against Japan. Fortunately, he was a quick study. He had to be, since he had skipped midlevel command positions altogether when he was promoted from lieutenant colonel to brigadier general immediately following the 1942 raid on Tokyo. Both Marshall and Arnold were witness to his rapid development as an air commander.

After the war had ended, Hap Arnold wrote to Jimmy that as a lieutenant, Doolittle had been a constant worry. He hastened to point out that as time passed, Doolittle grew into a high-quality leader. "Your skill as an airman, your ability as an aviation engineer, and finally your all-around aviation knowledge brought admiration of all who came in contact with you."[5] A high compliment and realization, particularly since at one time or another, Doolittle had received aggravated rebukes from Generals Eisenhower, Spaatz, and Arnold. He learned from his command mistakes and led the Eighth Air Force into battle over Europe during the critical months of the air war against Germany in early 1944. His fearless decision to detach escort fighters from the bomber formations, in an effort to successfully execute Arnold's orders to attack the Luftwaffe and sweep it from the sky, turned the tide of the battle for air supremacy before D day. Doolittle flew over the landing beachhead that day in a P-38 Lightning fighter plane. "One of my fondest dreams materialized," he wrote, "when I realized that German air opposition was virtually nil. I did not see a single enemy fighter."[6] He knew that he and his command had achieved their objective.

Jimmy always considered himself a fighter pilot—a free-spirited and rebellious fighter pilot at that. He began his flying career as a fighter-pilot instructor teaching aerial gunnery during the Great War. His achievements in racing, experimentation, and stunting and even to some degree in combat were accomplished while alone in an airplane. Noted exceptions were episodes of unauthorized wing-walking and many blind-landing flights with Ben Kelsey in the safety seat. He considered that fighters were different from bombers in that the former were individualistic loners harboring an inclination to "take the offensive."[7] These qualities have persisted through the years as part of the fighter-pilot mystique—an attitude that has been sought out as desirable for pilots of single-seat aircraft since before the First World War. This self-perception falls right in line with Doolittle's upbringing and development throughout his life and is largely responsible for much of his tremendous success.

In later years, Doolittle openly advocated a strong, technically advanced national military force. He believed that the "military establishment must be able to deter all-out war and must be able to cope with small wars that from time to time will be forced upon us. In order to have that, we have to have the support of science and technology because over a period of time what we have is going to become obsolete."[8] His longtime association with the science of aeronautics and the continued study of flight was deeply ingrained and was often reflected in postwar associations with the NACA and other scientific groups.

Beyond professional accomplishments, however, there were more personal achievements of which he was equally proud. The most significant of these remained, until the end, his eight-decade love affair with Joe, his wife. He closed his autobiography with this tribute to her: "The best thing I ever did was to convince Joe that she should marry me; the luckiest thing that ever happened to me was when she finally did. That's why, whenever I'm asked, I say that I would never want to relive my life. I could never be so lucky again."[9] He was probably right.

Notes

Chapter 1

1. James H. Doolittle with C. V. Glines, *I Could Never Be So Lucky Again* (New York: Bantam Books, 1991), 21. Much of Doolittle's early life story is derived from pages 15–66 in this well-written autobiography.
2. Doolittle family photo albums, National Air and Space Museum Archives, Washington, D.C.
3. Ibid.
4. Doolittle, *I Could Never Be So Lucky Again*, 24.
5. See Tom Crouch, *The Bishop's Boys* (New York: W.W. Norton & Company, 1989), Book Three: The World.
6. Doolittle, *I Could Never Be So Lucky Again*, 31, 58.
7. Ibid., 42.
8. Ibid., 45–46.
9. Ibid., 46–47.
10. Ibid., 50.
11. Ibid., 60.
12. Ibid., 56–61. In 1919, Doolittle pushed fuel calculations in an attempt to reach a distant destination. He was leading two other airplanes on this mission. He failed to realize that the consumption of fuel was not the same for each of the craft. His miscalculation left one plane short of the destination, a useless wreck.
13. Quoted in Glines, *Master of the Calculated Risk*, 42–43. Appeared in the *Los Angeles Times*, 25 and 26 November 1918.

Chapter 2

1. Doolittle, *I Could Never Be So Lucky Again*, 64.
2. Ibid., 66.

3. Ibid., 70; see also James H. Doolittle, USAF Oral History Program, 20 July 1967, USAF/HRA, Montgomery, AL, K239.0512-998, 2.

4. "Lieutenant Doolittle's Wonderful Feat," *Air Service News Letter* VI, no. 28 (October 10, 1922): 4.

5. "Doolittle's Hard Luck," *Air Service News Letter* VI, no. 26 (September 13, 1922): 2.

6. While flying west, a pilot actually lengthens his day by "chasing the sun." Hence, there are effectively three hours more daylight than darkness on this east-to-west flight.

7. "Lieutenant Doolittle's Wonderful Feat," 1–4. Flight times listed in the article for the flight were rounded but reflect essentially the same flight and total times as Doolittle's personal records; also "Air Service," *Aviation* (September 25, 1922): 389.

8. Doolittle, *I Could Never Be So Lucky Again*, 81.

9. Doolittle, USAF Oral History Program, 20 July 1967, K239.0512-998, 3–5.

10. Doolittle, *I Could Never Be So Lucky Again*. 86.

11. James H. Doolittle, "Wing Loads as Determined by the Accelerometer" (Master's Thesis, MIT, 1924), National Air and Space Museum Library (hereinafter NASM), Doolittle biographical file, CD 608500-1; also Doolittle, *I Could Never Be So Lucky Again*, 92–93.

12. Ibid., 95.

13. James H. Doolittle, "The Effect of the Wind Velocity Gradient on Airplane Performance" (Dr. of Sc. Dissertation, MIT, 1925), copy in NASM, CD 608500-4. Doolittle called it a doctor of science in aeronautical engineering, while other sources called it a doctor of aeronautical science. It really did not matter; his was one of the first degrees of its kind ever awarded by an American institution.

14. "The Schneider Cup Race," *Aviation* XIX, no. 18 (November 2, 1925): 620–628. The R3C-1 was the land version and the R3C-2 was the seaplane version. For a closer look at Mason Patrick, see Robert P. White, *Mason Patrick and the Fight for Air Service Independence* (Washington, D.C.: Smithsonian Institution Press, 2002).

15. Ibid., 620.

16. Doolittle, *I Could Never Be So Lucky Again*, 110–112.

17. Ibid., 115.

18. Ibid., 116.

19. James H. Doolittle, USAF Oral History Program, USAF/HRA, Maxwell AFB, AL, K239.0512-998, 8.

20. Transcript of interview of James H. Doolittle, N.D. On file at NASM, CD 608500-3, 19.

21. Doolittle, *I Could Never Be So Lucky Again*, 124. "The honor was much appreciated," Jimmy said.

Chapter 3

1. James H. Doolittle, "Early Blind Flying," *Aerospace Engineering* 20, no. 10 (October 1961).

2. Doolittle, *I Could Never Be So Lucky Again*, 132.

3. Richard P. Hallion, *Legacy of Flight* (Washington: University of Washington Press, 1977), 111; see also Doolittle, *I Could Never Be So Lucky Again*, 135; and James H. Doolittle, USAF Oral History Program, 20 July 1967, USAF/HRA, Maxwell AFB, AL, K239.0512-998, 5–7.

4. Doolittle, *I Could Never Be So Lucky Again*, 65, and 137–138.

5. James H. Doolittle. Preface to *The Dragon's Teeth?* by Benjamin S. Kelsey (Washington, D.C.: Smithsonian Institution Press, 1982); also Doolittle, "Early Blind Flying."

6. Doolittle, *I Could Never Be So Lucky Again*, 136–137.

7. Doolittle, *I Could Never Be So Lucky Again*, 143–146; and Hallion, *Legacy of Flight*, 119–120.

8. Doolittle, *I Could Never Be So Lucky Again*, 144.

9. Doolittle, "Early Blind Flying."

10. Quoted in Hallion, *Legacy of Flight*, 123; also see Doolittle, "Early Blind Flying," for throttle details.

11. Kelsey, *The Dragon's Teeth?*, 38.

12. "Simulated Landings, Take-Offs in Fog Made by Lieut. Doolittle," *Aviation* (October 5, 1929), 718.

13. James H. Doolittle interview transcript, N.D., NASM, Doolittle biographical file, CD 608500-3; see also Doolittle, interviewed by Leish, April 1960, USAF/HRA, 146.34-39, 15–16.

14. See Rebecca Hancock Cameron, *Training to Fly: Military Flight Training, 1907–1945* (Washington, D.C.: Air Force History and Museums Program), 264–267; also Doolittle, *I Could Never Be So Lucky Again*, 152.

15. Doolittle interview transcript, N.D., NASM, Doolittle biographical file, CD 608500–3, 24. Jimmy's and Joe's mothers both died shortly thereafter.

Chapter 4

1. Doolittle, *I Could Never Be So Lucky Again,* 164. The *New York Times* ran the story, which was logical, as the event occurred at Mitchel Field, Long Island.
2. Ibid., 166–167.
3. Ibid., 168–171.
4. Ibid., 182.
5. Doolittle interview, NASM, 17.
6. Ibid., 18.
7. Glines summarizes the importance on 100-octane in *Master of the Calculated Risk,* 176–177. It wasn't until 1942 that the distinction of octane change with changes of engine power became fully appreciated. The 80/87 and 100/130 numbers of today's fuels reflect this discovery. High-octane fuels allowed engines to use less fuel for more economical operation and longer range with no increase in temperatures. Water injection allowed even more power over the short term.
8. Tom Crouch, "Centennial of Flight," draft manuscript, National Air and Space Museum, 2002.
9. Doolittle, *I Could Never Be So Lucky Again,* 199.
10. Ibid., 200.
11. Ibid, 199–200.
12. Any one of these infractions today, by civil or military pilots, usually results in abrupt and irreversible loss of a pilot's "ticket." It is said that for every flight regulation there is a dead pilot who caused it.
13. Doolittle, *I Could Never Be So Lucky Again,* 208.
14. Ibid., 212–214.
15. Jimmy Doolittle, interviewed by Mr. Leish, April 1960, USAF/HRA, 146.34-39, 23.
16. Doolittle, *I Could Never Be So Lucky Again,* 215.
17. Doolittle transcript, NASM, 9.
18. H. H. Arnold, "Airplanes, Less Engines, Including Airplane Propellers and Airplane Parachutes: A Study Prepared by the Air Service, 1922," located in the Robert Arnold Collection,

Sonoma, California. For context, see Dik A. Daso, *Hap
Arnold and the Evolution of American Airpower*, (Washington,
D. C.: Smithsonian Institution Press, 2000) 87–89.

19. Fifty thousand airplanes speech in Eugene M. Emme, ed., *The
Impact of Air Power* (Princeton, N.J.: D. Van Nostrand, 1959),
69.

Chapter 5

1. Col. Robert G. Emmens, Speech given at the National Air and
Space Museum, CD/ROM, 8 December 1983. One might only
imagine that the feeling prevalent in America after the Japanese
attack on Pearl Harbor approached the swell of emotions that
enveloped the United States immediately following the tragic
events of 9/11.

2. Gen. Arnold made notes during a 28 January 1942 meeting with
FDR. During that meeting, the president insisted that "from a
psychological standpoint . . . it was most important to bomb
Japan as soon as possible."

3. James H. Doolittle to Commanding General of the Army Air
Forces, "Report on the Aerial Bombing of Japan," 5 June 1942.
NASM CD 608500-3, 1. Two flew off the carrier; the third one
was a spare.

4. James H. Doolittle, interviewed by Murray Green, Los Angeles,
California, 22 December 1977, located in the USAF Academy
Special Collections, Hap Arnold (Murray Green Collection), 10.

5. Carroll V. Glines, *Doolittle's Tokyo Raiders* (Princeton, N.J.:
C. Van Nostrand, 1964), 28.

6. Ibid., 23, and 36; see also C. V. Glines, *The Doolittle Raid:
America's Daring First Strike against Japan* (New York: Orion
Books, 1980), 50–51.

7. Emmens, 8 December 1983; also Doolittle, "Report to CGAAF,"
2, 9; also see Glines, *Doolittle's Tokyo Raiders*, 7, and 42. The
commanding officer for the Eighty-ninth, Maj. John A. Hilger,
was selected as Doolittle's deputy commander.

8. "Policy Covering AAF Security Classification and Selected Data
on Aircraft and Equipment," Headquarters Army Air Forces,
Washington, D.C., March 1945, 15. Although the data are for
later models of the B-25, the basic ranges were about the same in
all models.

9. There is some confusion as to whether Doolittle is including eight gas cans that were added to each aircraft at the last minute while on the deck of the *Hornet.* Emmens, 8 December 1983. Doolittle's notes are reproduced in Glines, *Doolittle's Tokyo Raiders,* 37–41; also see Glines, *The Doolittle Raid,* 32–33.

10. The evolution of bombsights is detailed in Stephen L. McFarland's *America's Pursuit of Precision Bombing, 1910–1945* (Washington, D.C.: Smithsonian Institution Press, 1995).

11. Doolittle, "Report to CGAAF," 7–8.

12. Today, aux. #9 is Hurlburt Air Force Base, the home of Air Force Special Operations.

13. Doolittle, "Report to CGAAF," 10.

14. Glines, *Doolittle's Tokyo Raiders,* 35.

15. Emmens, 8 December 1983.

16. Doolittle, interviewed by Murray Green, 22 December 1977, 8.

17. Dik A. Daso, *Hap Arnold and the Evolution of American Airpower* (Washington, D.C.: Smithsonian Institution Press, 2000), 172.

18. Glines, *The Doolittle Raid,* 48–51.

19. Glines, *Doolittle's Tokyo Raiders,* 61–62; Doolittle, "Report to CGAAF," 12. In his original planning notes, Doolittle wanted each pilot to complete at least one actual carrier takeoff.

20. Glines, *Doolittle's Tokyo Raiders,* 73.

21. Glines, *The Doolittle Raid,* 45. As related to Glines by the Doolittles themselves; also see Doolittle, *I Could Never Be So Lucky Again,* 258.

22. Recollections vary as to when the announcement was actually made, from that same afternoon to three days later.

23. GE Lecture Series, National Air and Space Museum, 9 April 1992. Col. Joseph W. Manske comments.

24. During anything but perfectly calm seas, the ridiculous folly of a game of pool in rough seas was obvious. In defense of the ship's morale officer, carriers were very large ships and very stable under most sea conditions.

25. Doolittle, "Report to CGAAF," 14.

26. Glines, *Doolittle's Tokyo Raiders,* 66–67. This was one day later than originally planned.

27. Doolittle, "Report to CGAAF," 14.

28. James H. Doolittle, USAF Oral History Program, 20 July 1967, K239.0512-998, AFHRC, Maxwell AFB, AL, 11.

29. Doolittle, interviewed by Murray Green, 22 December 1977, 11.

30. Glines, *Doolittle's Tokyo Raiders*, 118.

31. Emmens, Speech given at the National Air and Space Museum, CD/ROM, 8 December 1983.

32. Doolittle, "Report to CGAAF," 15; GE Lecture Series, National Air and Space Museum, 9 April 1992. During the question- and-answer period of the event, those on the panel, Maj. Gen. David M. Jones, Col. Joseph W. Manske, Lt. Col. Richard E. Cole, and Lt. Col. Robert L. Hite confirmed that the landing plan for their situation did not exist. Some accounts note the takeoff time as 0818.

33. Doolittle, "Report to CGAAF," 15.

34. The number 16 B-25 had also received minor damage to its front windscreen when its nose was bumped by the ground crew during repositioning.

35. Doolittle, "Report to CGAAF," 17.

36. GE Lecture Series, National Air and Space Museum, 9 April 1992.

37. Carl von Clausewitz, *On War,* indexed edition, edited and translated by Michael Howard and Peter Paret (Princeton, N.J.: Princeton University Press, 1984), 119.

38. Doolittle, interviewed by Murray Green, 22 December 1977, 13.

39. Glines, *Doolittle's Tokyo Raiders*, 142–143, 178–179, 188, 264. Reproduced here are mission accounts provided by the crewmen who flew the mission.

40. Doolittle, "Report to CGAAF," 16.

41. GE Lecture Series, National Air and Space Museum, 9 April 1992; also Doolittle, "Report to CGAAF," 18.

42. GE Lecture Series, National Air and Space Museum, 9 April 1992.

43. Emmens, 8 December 1983; see also Glines, *Doolittle's Tokyo Raiders,* 212. York's finely tuned carburetors were supposedly removed and replaced at Sacramento but the untuned and less fuel-efficient parts were not detected until on board the *Hornet.* This accounted for the gross disparity in fuel consumption.

44. Doolittle, "Report to CGAAF," 20. Doolittle omitted the number eight crew landing in Russia in the body of the report, but in the detailed account for each aircraft, the details of the landing are mentioned on page 25.

45. Glines, *Doolittle's Tokyo Raiders*, 88.

46. Based upon Col. Merian C. Cooper's 22 June 1942 report to the commanding general on the Doolittle Raid. Quoted in Glines, *Doolittle's Tokyo Raiders*, 101.

47. GE Lecture Series, National Air and Space Museum, 9 April 1992. Cole's comments.

48. Birch was killed on 25 August 1945 by Chinese Communists. The John Birch Society, a vocal postwar anti-Communist group, bears his name.

49. Doolittle, *I Could Never Be So Lucky Again*, 277–278.

50. Ibid., 282. Also spelled Yung-Hui; Doolittle received the award Class III; Hilger received the award Class IV.

51. Michael S. Sherry, *The Rise of American Air Power* (New Haven, Conn.: Yale University Press, 1987), 122–125. Popular cartoon media frequently characterized the Japanese as animals, often cowardly, and always under attack by a powerful representation of American might—usually a soaring eagle.

52. From a National Archives photo of one of the Raiders' loaded bomb bays, reprinted in N. L. Avery, *B-25 Mitchell: The Magnificent Medium* (St. Paul, Minn.: Phalanx Publishing, 1992), 92.

53. Glines, *Doolittle's Tokyo Raiders*, 137–139. Although presented on 19 May, the official date on General Order 29, the order for Doolittle's Medal of Honor, is 9 June 1942.

Chapter 6

1. Reproduced in Doolittle, *I Could Never Be So Lucky Again*, 291.

2. Walter Lord, *Incredible Victory* (New York: Harper & Row, 1967), 5.

3. Richard G. Davis, "Take Down That Damn Sign!" *Air Power History* 40, no. 4 (Winter 1993), 17; see also World War II Information Fact Sheets (Washington, D.C.: 50th Anniversary of WWII Commemorative Committee, 1995). Some estimates for Japanese losses reached 2,500, since the total complement of the Kaga was never accurately determined.

4. Quoted in Thomas E. Griffith Jr., *MacArthur's Airman* (Lawrence, Kans.: University Press of Kansas, 1998), 52.

5. Actor George C. Scott in the film *Patton* immortalized this famous speech, reprinted in Doolittle, *I Could Never Be So Lucky Again.*

6. James H. Doolittle, interviewed by Murray Green, 22 December 1977, Los Angeles, USAF Academy Special Collections, 14–15.

7. Marshall to Eisenhower, 14 September 1942, National Archives, item 744, CM-OUT 4695, 14 September 1942, OPD TS message file.

8. Dwight D. Eisenhower, *Crusade in Europe* (Garden City, N.Y.: Doubleday, 1948), 122.

9. W. F. Craven and J. L. Cate, *The Army Air Forces in World War II*, Vol. II (Washington, D.C.: Office of Air Force History, New Imprint, 1983), 51–52.

10. Doolittle, *I Could Never Be So Lucky Again,* 302–303.

11. Ibid., 308–309.

12. Craven and Cate, Vol. II, 58–59.

13. Doolittle, *I Could Never Be So Lucky Again,* 319.

14. The Reminiscences of James H. Doolittle, April 1960, p. 29, in the Oral History Collection of Columbia University.

15. From an old poem in the 97th Bomb Group war diary.

16. Doolittle, *I Could Never Be So Lucky Again,* 340–341.

17. Craven and Cate, Vol. II, 161–165, 416–417.

18. Craven and Cate, Vol. II, 161–165.

19. Doolittle, *I Could Never Be So Lucky Again,* 331 and 341.

20. Quoted in Dik A. Daso, *Hap Arnold and the Evolution of American Airpower* (Washington, D.C.: Smithsonian Institution Press, 2000), 201.

21. Doolittle, *I Could Never Be So Lucky Again,* 349.

22. Craven and Cate, Vol. II, 566–569.

23. Doolittle, *I Could Never Be So Lucky Again,* 369–370.

24. Ralph H. Nutter, *With the Possum and the Eagle, The Memoir of a Navigator's War over Germany and Japan* (Novato, Calif.: Presidio, 2002), 123.

25. Craven and Cate, Vol. II, 745–746.

26. James Parton, *Air Force Spoken Here* (Bethesda, Md.: Adler & Adler, 1986), 338. Parton's examination of the events surrounding

Eaker's transfer is by far the most detailed and descriptive of any source on the subject.

27. Parton, *Air Force Spoken Here*, 333–343. Doolittle supposed that he had simply been moved as part of the Spaatz move. Ike was comfortable with Spaatz; Doolittle did not have the rank to fill the Mediterranean slot. Doolittle, interviewed by Murray Green, 22 December 1977, 15.

28. Reprinted in Glenn Infield, *Big Week* (Washington, D.C.: Brassey's [U.S.], 1974), 27–28.

Chapter 7

1. The official AAF history of WWII dedicates an entire nine-hundred-page volume to the story that will be broadly summarized in the next several pages. Many books have been written about one aspect or another of this air campaign and should be consulted for detailed examination of specific aspects of the European air war.

2. The Reminiscences of James H. Doolittle, April 1960, p. 33, in the Oral History Collection of Columbia University; see also, Doolittle, *I Could Never Be So Lucky Again*, 379–380.

3. Quoted in Richard G. Davis, "Take Down That Damned Sign!" *Airpower History* 40, no. 4, (Winter 1993), 19.

4. James H. Doolittle, interviewed by Murray Green, 22 December 1977, Los Angeles, California, USAF Academy Special Collections, 17–18; see also Doolittle, 377 and 381.

5. The Reminiscences of James H. Doolittle, April 1960, p. 30, in the Oral History Collection of Columbia University.

6. Glenn Infield, *Big Week* (Washington, D.C.: Brassey's [U.S.], 1976), 32. Infield notes that Oboe was also occasionally used during these raids.

7. For a fresh, lively, and detailed examination of CBO bombardment doctrine, see Robin Neillands, *The Bomber War* (New York: The Overlook Press, 2001), chapters 12 and 13.

8. Quoted in Doolittle, *I Could Never Be So Lucky Again*, 394.

9. Infield, *Big Week*, 45–46.

10. Craven and Cate, Vol. III, 33.

11. Neillands, *The Bomber War*, 299.

12. Craven and Cate, Vol. III, 45–46.

13. Richard G. Davis, *Carl A. Spaatz and the Air War in Europe* (Washington D.C.: Center for Air Force History, 1993), 321–323. On 23 February, the weather precluded launching any missions; also Doolittle, *I Could Never Be So Lucky Again*, 395.

14. Neillands, *The Bomber War*, 299–300.

15. Doolittle, *I Could Never Be So Lucky Again*, 396 and 399.

16. Ibid., 396–397.

17. Craven and Cate, Vol. III, 51.

18. Reminiscences of James H. Doolittle, April 1960, p. 31.

19. Ibid., 33–34.

20. Doolittle, *I Could Never Be So Lucky Again*, 399.

21. Dik A. Daso, *Hap Arnold and the Evolution of American Airpower* (Washington, D.C.: Smithsonian Institution Press, 2000), 185–188; also see Craven and Cate, Vol. III, 530–532.

22. During the Persian Gulf War (1991), American air forces employed precision-guided weapons that had their foundations in this type of experimentation during WWII.

23. Doolittle, *I Could Never Be So Lucky Again*, 401; see also Craven and Cate, Vol. III, 163–164.

24. Daso, *Hap Arnold*, 1.

25. Doolittle, *I Could Never Be So Lucky Again*, 404.

26. Figures are taken from Craven and Cate, Vol. III, 233–234, and Edward C. Mann III, *Thunder and Lightning* (Montgomery, Ala.: Air University Press, 1995), 11–12.

27. Quoted in Doolittle, *I Could Never Be So Lucky Again*, 406.

28. Craven and Cate, Vol. III, 658–662; also see Doolittle, 415–417.

29. Craven and Cate, Vol. III, 536–537.

30. Doolittle, *I Could Never Be So Lucky Again*, 424–427.

31. Richard J. Overy, *Why the Allies Won* (New York: W.W. Norton, 1996), 124–125.

32. Craven and Cate, Vol. III, 657–660.

33. Doolittle, *I Could Never Be So Lucky Again*, 435.

34. Doolittle, interviewed by Murray Green, 22 December 1977, Doolittle was originally destined for Air Materiel Command after his tour in Europe, but he asked to go to Okinawa with his Eighth Air Force instead. Arnold acquiesced but not before verbally lambasting Jimmy for asking not to be assigned under General Stillwell, as Arnold had suggested.

Chapter 8

1. Carlo D'Este, *Patton* (New York: HarperCollins, 1995), 748; see also Doolittle, *I Could Never Be So Lucky Again,* 442.

2. Richard Rhodes, *The Making of the Atomic Bomb* (New York: Touchstone, 1986), 667. The Trinity test was accomplished on the morning of 16 July 1945 in the desert near Alamogordo, New Mexico.

3. Doolittle, *I Could Never Be So Lucky Again,* 454; see also Doolittle, *Impact,* Book 6, xviii.

4. Werrell, *Blankets of Fire,* 222; see also Doolittle, *Impact,* Book 6, xiii.

5. Carroll V. Glines, *Four Came Home* (Princeton, N.J.: D. Van Nostrand, 1966); and *Doolittle's Tokyo Raiders* (Princeton, N.J.: D. Van Nostrand 1964). Colonel Glines, the Raiders' official historian, wrote several books concerning Doolittle, the Raid, and the men.

6. Doolittle, *I Could Never Be So Lucky Again,* 467.

7. Quoted in Daso, *Hap Arnold,* 172.

8. James H. Straubel, *Crusade for Airpower* (Washington, D.C.: Aerospace Education Foundation, 1982), 32–33.

9. Quoted in Straubel, *Crusade for Airpower,* 36.

10. Quoted in Doolittle, *I Could Never Be So Lucky Again,* 479–480.

11. Walter J. Boyne, *A History of the U.S. Air Force, 1947–1997* (New York: St. Martin's Press, 1997), 32–38.

12. Quoted in Straubel, *Crusade for Airpower,* 38; Hap Arnold felt the same way and voiced his concerns about the lack of unified air command to Secretary of Defense Louis Johnson only four days before he died in 1950.

13. Doolittle, *I Could Never Be So Lucky Again,* 488.

14. Bernard A. Schriever, "Reminiscences: Doolittle and Post–World War II Research and Development," in *Air Power History* (Winter 1993), 27.

15. Quoted in Dik A. Daso, *Architects of American Air Supremacy* (Maxwell AFB, Ala.: Air University Press, 1996), 165–166. Doolittle also participated in the Anderson Committee immediately following this report. It convened at Maxwell AFB and contributed the administrative backbone to the Ridenour concept.

16. Doolittle, *I Could Never Be So Lucky Again,* 510–511

17. Ibid., 494.

18. Alex Roland, *Model Research*, Vol. 1 (Washington, D.C.: National Air and Space Administration, 1984), 284.

19. James H. Doolittle, interviewed by Eugene M. Emme and W. D. Putnam, 21 April 1969, NASA Archives, Washington, D.C., 4.

20. Schriever, "Reminiscences: Doolittle and Post–World War II Research and Development," 27.

21. William F. Trimble, *Jerome Hunsaker and the Rise of American Aeronautics* (Washington, D.C.: Smithsonian Institution Press, 2002), 198–199; see also Doolittle, *I Could Never Be So Lucky Again*, 496–501.

22. Geoffrey Perret, *Eisenhower* (New York: Random House, 1997), 476–477.

23. Doolittle, *I Could Never Be So Lucky Again*, 522.

Chapter 9

1. Doolittle, *I Could Never Be So Lucky Again*, 527.

2. Herman S. Wolk, "Renaissance Man of Aviation," in *Air Power History* (Winter 1993), 4–8.

3. Doolittle, *I Could Never Be So Lucky Again*, 530–531.

4. Ibid., 533–535.

5. Ibid., quoted on page 60.

6. James H. Doolittle, "Daylight Precision Bombing," in *Impact*, book 6 (New York: James Parton Co., 1980) xii–xviii.

7. Ibid., xiv; see also Doolittle, *I Could Never Be So Lucky Again*, 52.

8. James H. Doolittle, interviewed by E. Emme and W. Putnam, 21 April 1969, NASA Archives, Washington, D.C., 68A, 51–53.

9. Doolittle, *I Could Never Be So Lucky Again*, 539.

Bibliographic Note

The purpose of this bibliographic note is to tell readers who want to know more about Doolittle where to look. No attempt has been made to list every work cited in the endnotes or used in writing this book.

The best starting place is Doolittle's autobiography, *I Could Never Be So Lucky Again* (New York: Bantam Books, 1991), written with Carroll V. Glines, historian for the Doolittle Raiders. This work lends Doolittle's personal flavor to an account of a lifetime of adventure and involvement in the technological development of aeronautics in America. Glines has written several other books and articles on Doolittle and the Raid.

Other authors have also written about the Tokyo Raid. Three of their books are James M. Merrill's *Target Tokyo: The Halsey-Doolittle Raid* (Chicago: Rand McNally, 1964), Duane P. Schultz's *The Doolittle Raid* (New York: St. Martin's Press, 1988), and the most recent Craig Nelson's *The First Heroes* (New York: Viking, 2002). Merrill's book emphasizes the role played by Halsey's naval forces in executing the raid, while Shultz's work, a solid compilation of the available material, is geared more to the nonhistorian and omits the traditional academic endnotes.

Although some have been critical of his work, Nelson has written an entertaining, balanced, and generally accurate account of the Raid. Sporting an openly journalistic style, this book brings Doolittle's daring adventure to life in Technicolor while presenting the historic background surrounding the events clearly. The emotional highs are majestic, while the candid brutality recounting the details of events such as the rape of

Nanking lays wide open the context under which most Americans developed their attitudes toward the Japanese as less than human. His is the only book that attempts to contextualize the raid in the broadest of terms.

All of these books draw upon essentially the same group of secondary sources and most of the same primary documents, including official mission reports and military and presidential staff memos. Oral interviews are plentiful, especially in Nelson, as all of the Raiders who were willing have been interviewed several times. These transcriptions are available from many library collections, from Columbia University to the USAF Academy. Primary materials from the Library of Congress, the National Archives, and military service archives are also available.

Some of the most interesting material concerning Doolittle was written by Doolittle. His technical papers (his master's thesis, dissertation, and military technical reports) define the depth of his aeronautical scientific knowledge. His family photo album documents a lifetime of antics and achievements beyond those of an average American family. Many of these are available at the National Air and Space Museum archives division; others can be found in the Doolittle Library at the University of Texas at Dallas.

Again, the pen of Carroll "CV" Glines provides biographical works on Jimmy Doolittle. These include *Jimmy Doolittle: Daredevil Aviator and Scientist* (New York: Macmillan, 1972) and *Jimmy Doolittle: Master of the Calculated Risk* (New York: Van Nostrand Reinhold, 1980). Although others have attempted biographical works, Glines's, admittedly biased toward the general, are incomplete, since all were published several years before Doolittle's death.

For those beginning their studies of American military history in the Second World War, efforts should always be made to consult the official service histories where they apply: the Army's "Green Books," the U.S. Army Air Forces' seven-volume set (generally referred to as "Craven & Cate," the authors), and Samuel Eliot Morison's fifteen-volume history of WWII naval operations. In these gems are solid history and a wealth of primary-source information seldom found elsewhere.

Doolittle's personal and military papers are located in several locations: the Library of Congress, the National Archives, the USAF Historical Research Center at Maxwell AFB, the USAF Academy Special Collections Branch, and the Doolittle Library (Eugene McDermott Library, Special Collections Department) at the University of Texas at Dallas. Other Doolittle-related materials are located in various naval archives (concerning the Raid) and in the collections about the Shell Oil Company and the employees of that firm. The archives of the committees upon which Doolittle served also contain letters and papers related to his service. The USAF Scientific Advisory Board, for example, has reports and memos related to his years as chairman.

Because of the breadth of Doolittle's acquaintances over nine decades, there are likely to be Doolittle letters in the files of many aviation personalities and business executives. His dealings with the Royal Air Force are a case in point, as he worked with them while a civilian at Shell and also as a military commander during the Second World War.

Index

About the Author

Dik Alan Daso (B.S., USAF Academy; M.A., Ph.D., University of South Carolina) is the curator of modern military aircraft at the Smithsonian Institution, National Air and Space Museum, Washington, D.C. A retired Air Force lieutenant colonel, he has served as an RF-4C "Phantom" instructor pilot; an F-15 "Eagle" pilot; twice as a T-38 "Talon" instructor pilot; an instructor of history at the USAF Academy; and the chief of Air Force doctrine at Headquarters Air Force, Pentagon. During his career, Daso accumulated more than 2,700 flying hours. He contributed a chapter to *The Air Force,* an illustrated history of that service. Daso has also written two books: *Architects of American Air Supremacy: Gen. Hap Arnold and Dr. Theodore von Kármán* (Maxwell AFB, Alabama: Air University Press, 1997) and *Hap Arnold and the Evolution of American Airpower* (Washington, D.C.: Smithsonian Institution Press, 2000), which won the 2001 American Institute of Aeronautics and Astronautics (AIAA) History Manuscript Award.

MILITARY PROFILES
AVAILABLE

MILITARY PROFILES
FORTHCOMING
Meade
Richard A. Sauers
Halsey
Robert J. Cressman
Rickover
Thomas B. Allen and Norman Polmar
Tirpitz
Michael Epkenhans

DATE DUE		
JA25 '05		
FEB 24 08		

DISCARDED